The Quest
for Wholeness

The Quest for Wholeness

MARTIN ISRAEL

Darton, Longman and Todd
London

First published in 1989 by
Darton, Longman and Todd Ltd
89 Lillie Road, London SW6 1UD

British Library Cataloguing in Publication Data

Israel, Martin, *1927–*
    The quest for wholeness
    1. Christianity. Spiritual healing
    I. Title
    615.8'52
    ISBN 0–232–51756–8

Phototypeset by Input Typesetting Ltd, London SW19 8DR
Printed and bound in Great Britain by Anchor Press Ltd, Tiptree, Essex

Dedicated to the memory of
Mary, Constance and Ronald

Contents

I have come that men may have life, and have it in all its fullness.

John 10:10

So shall we all at last attain to the unity inherent in our faith and our knowledge of the Son of God – to mature manhood, measured by nothing less than the full stature of Christ.

Ephesians 4:13

Prologue

'One further warning, my son: the use of books is endless, and much study is wearisome.' This observation, from Ecclesiastes 12:12, reminds me of the vast literature about the ministry of healing currently available and being augmented year by year. The Church's ministry of healing is now an integral part of its work, but in fact all worship has within it a healing potential.

To me, healing is the process whereby humanity is gradually restored to the divine image in which it was created so that we all can come to share in the very being of God. This vision may be simplistically impractical when we remember the unfortunate people born with severe physical and mental defects, to say nothing of the terrible family and communal circumstances in which many others are reared. While everything possible must be done to relieve suffering, the human condition contains within its core an innate nobility that is here to triumph over adversity and to assert its deeper divinity so emphatically as to work towards the lifting up of the entire world to eternal glory. It is a privilege as well as a responsibility to be born human, and full healing involves more than a surface amelioration of suffering, essential as this may be in the short term. In fact, the process of life is one of progressive healing, and we have ultimately to find the tools of health in the circumstances around us, unpromising as these often appear to be. Awareness of the present moment

1

is the secret of the healing ministry. This is a sensitivity to the universal thrust of life, which may to some extent be identified with God in religious parlance, and to our fellow-creatures also.

What the world dismisses as a failure in healing may be a future instance of glowing success in a sufferer's life. What may seem to be an amazing healing of a diseased person could, on the other hand, be the means of his stultification if he becomes fanatically entrenched in a particular line of thought that can admit no other possibilities of truth.

Life is seldom comfortable for any length of time if we are doing our work properly. But its end is well worth while: to find freedom from material and psychological illusion, to enter into the depths of our own being, and to know the Divine Presence that will never leave us alone until we are fully ourselves in the heart of reality. It is there that we know God as he is.

All the cases recorded in this book are real, but the names of the people mentioned have been changed – with the exception of the three to whom the book is dedicated. Though I owe much to the witness of these three and am dedicated to their memory, I have not refrained from drawing attention to their failings as ministers of healing. When one speaks of departed friends, it is all too easy to embellish their images with an aura of infallibility and sanctity. In the same way, less scrupulous biographers can uncover less attractive aspects of their subjects in order to create a sensation. As Shakespeare wrote in *Julius Caesar*, 'The evil that men do lives after them; the good is oft interred with their bones'. And Dostoevsky noted in *The Brothers Karamazov*, in relation to the unexpectedly early putrefaction of the body of the saintly Father Zosima and the scandal it evoked among the bystanders, that nothing is more pleasant than witnessing the humiliation of a good person – at least for the common run of humanity who always feel challenged by the apparent holiness of one of their number. The behaviour of most of those who witnessed the Crucifixion reinforces this observation.

I have tried to steer a middle course between these two

extremes. It is important for us all to recognize that no one, other than Christ, has attained wholeness. The minister of healing works towards that end no less in helping others to health than in the course of his or her everyday life. It is one thing to have a healing gift, but another to be fully healed oneself.

1

The Healing Experience

It was a warm, sunny summer day in August 1962 when I
entered the portals of a church in Brighton situated close to
the sea-front. A life-long sufferer from hay fever, this
particular year I had seen the worst of my affliction. It was
the intractable blockage of my nose that provided the major
part of my distress: being an habitual nose-breather, I had
considerable difficulty in sleeping, since I found it well-nigh
impossible to keep my mouth continuously open as an alternative passage for air to and from the lungs. To assuage the
distress I had tried various remedies; a nose-spray was best,
but provided only temporary relief.

The cool tranquillity of the church contrasted with the
bright heat and the noisy traffic outside. I sat in a pew near
the front, in company with about twenty other people as we
awaited the ministrations of Constance Peters. She had served
in the ministry of healing for many years, having been licensed
by the Bishop of Chichester to perform her work in the ambit
of the Church. As we waited, I glanced at my watch: it was
about 2 p.m. and I had an appointment in London at 4.30
p.m. And then the service commenced. It was extremely
simple, for the congregation were nearly all members of the
Fellowship that Constance had founded and so knew the
proceedings quite well.

After a hymn and some prayers, she proceeded to move
around the church, laying her hands on each of us in turn –

all sitting in the pews rather than kneeling at the altar-rail. Very soon my impatience mounted at the length of time she took over each person; if she continued at that rate I would certainly not be able to arrive at my destination in time! My agitation slowly intensified, and I nearly yielded to the temptation of quitting the service and driving back to London at once. It was courtesy rather than piety that kept me sitting in my pew. As Constance came to me, an inner voice told me to relax completely, and as I obeyed, I felt the presence of her hands over the top of my head. She did not appear to effect direct contact; rather, a warm vibration seemed to flow from her hands and penetrate through my scalp to the very centre of my head, clearing all blockages whether physical or spiritual. It was as if an electric radiator were operating directly above my head. The power that seemed to pour from Constance's hands was of shattering intensity; at once I felt my running nose dry up and the obstruction to free breathing slacken and abate.

After Constance had ended her ministry to each one of us, the priest in charge of the church laid his hands on us also – it was a cold, clammy touch devoid of any manifest healing radiation. As soon as the service had ended, having given heartfelt thanks to Constance and the priest, I drove back to London, arriving in time for my next appointment. An important aspect of this episode was my mental and emotional distance from the healing: until the very last moment, when I submitted in humble faith, allowing God to work his own healing in me. There was no question of 'suggestion', the insinuation of a belief or impulse into the mind of a credulous or gullible person, such as occurs classically under hypnosis but is also seen in mass rallies where there is a fervent emotional or religious current issuing from a directing master figure. My mind was engaged in considering the difficult journey ahead of me, not the healing power of God. The experience was indeed one of grace, an unmerited favour of God, that led to the completely unexpected amelioration of a physical handicap and a new directive in my life. Indeed, this experience was to prove crucial to the establishment of a healing ministry that I was soon to undertake.

The hay fever never returned with such vehemence, though the hypersensitivity to certain pollens persisted, albeit at a greatly reduced intensity. Above all, the nasal obstructive element of the condition subsided, so that I was able to breathe comfortably and sleep far more soundly than I had throughout many previous summers. In other words, there was an amazing improvement which was sustained, but not a complete cure. With the passage of years there has been a fine stabilization; there are only slight symptoms in the summer. Of course, I am aware that some allergic conditions do tend to lessen in severity with the ageing process, but the dramatic healing I received that afternoon showed me quite clearly that a higher spiritual healing was superimposed upon the healing power inherent in the body.

It was noteworthy also that the priest by whose courtesy the healing service took place in the precincts of his church, possessed no obvious gift himself. If anything, I would judge that he would dampen rather than ignite the healing fire of God, despite his ordination. Spiritual gifts are conferred in ways that we do not understand, so that no one can give an authoritative explanation of any particular phenomenon.

About a year later I attended another healing service conducted by Constance, and this time I was conscious of no special emanation despite my full awareness and outflowing faith. It was evident, as Constance herself told me, that my healing was a unique event. It occurred on one occasion, and for me only. I doubt whether any of the other members of that congregation at the Brighton church felt anything special or came away aware of being unusually blessed. But no doubt a deeper healing grace was bestowed on all of them so that they were more able to cope with their individual problems day by day than they had been previously.

This less spectacular element in healing is seldom considered, since its dividends are less immediate and no great benefit appears to accrue, at least in the short term. Furthermore, they do not boost the ego of the healer, nor do they serve to prove the existence of God in any tangible way. A generation that looks for signs, as Jesus implied, may arrive with nothing substantial but only voluminous froth. The ultimate sign will be that of Jonah, whose ministry produced a change in heart of his audience, the pagan Ninevites, and whose survival in the belly of the sea-monster prefigured the resurrection of Christ (Luke 11: 29–32 and Matthew 12: 38–41).

This thought brings us to consider a deeper type of healing, one primarily involving the soul, by which I mean the inner self that shows itself in decisions of moral and aesthetic value. I think here of another great friend, Mary Macaulay. A Canadian by birth, she served in Europe during the First World War. She then returned to America, where she undertook social work, all the time consorting with sources of spiritual enlightenment far beyond the scope of her secular field of activity. She was seeking some deeper understanding of the unhappiness so constantly encountered in the people she was assisting. Later on she came back to England, where she was in demand as a lecturer on normal psychological development. She spoke to women's groups, older schoolchildren, religious organizations and training colleges. She did not hesitate to proclaim her faith in the essentially spiritual nature of the human being. This point of view placed her somewhat out of court with the academic establishment of that time, while her open, eclectic view of spirituality – now taken largely for granted except in fundamentalistic quarters – failed to satisfy the complacent assurance of the pious. Her approach certainly went beyond the limits of speculation countenanced in conventional secular society. The acceptable landmarks of debate so easily solidify into walls that serve to reassure the complacent type of person in his or her intellectual prison, and Mary was set to extend these points of departure.

And so this courageous woman remained an outsider, a voice crying out in the wilderness of a social order poised between an arrogant agnosticism and a religious triumphalism. In due course she founded an adult education centre of her own where she could teach and counsel without interference. She was supported by a loyal group of followers, undistinguished academically and socially, but dedicated to her work. While her lectures were often applauded by people in greater authority, these – despite immediate promises – did nothing to further her work.

I came into contact with her a few years before the healing experience in Brighton I have already described. At that time I was in a state of despondency. My own peculiar insights into reality seemed to be at such variance with those of the medical establishment of which I was a member – the desire to enter heterodox fields was, and still is, basically alien to my way of life – that I doubted whether there was any substantial future ahead of me. Still young, I could not bear to envisage a future of dull compliance on the lower rungs of the professional ladder, for I knew only too well that I was most unlikely to rise to any position of professional significance, and only the loneliness of futility lay in store for me. I had been told of Mary's lectures by someone who lived in the same house as I, and so I went with trepidation as well as curiosity. I need not have been afraid, for the atmosphere of the room in which she was speaking had a calm assurance about it that I had never encountered in my professional or social life. Mary flowed out in a wisdom that far transcended mere intellectual brilliance; she spoke from the soul (whose bodily counterpart is, perhaps, the heart) rather than merely the head. I was accepted as I was, a fellow-human being with gifts unique to my particular identity for the destiny in store for me.

Though fields of speculation concerning the origin and destination of the human soul were fully explored – and the mystery of creation cannot be solved until we have been enabled to move beyond creature form to spiritual essence – I knew I was in the right milieu for further advancement of knowledge as well as actualization of my own personality. Yet none of the small audience could be termed intellectual; they were concerned about the welfare of their own family or the meaning behind their own travail. No categorical answer was – indeed, could in truth be – forthcoming, since we were all, including Mary herself, merely sojourners on the way of mortality whose end is death and becoming. And yet the simple ignorance was enfolded in a love so great that we all, including Mary, were lifted to a sphere of understanding that

8

made the views of the agnostic world a morass of learned ignorance. It was interesting that the teaching was basically common sense illuminated by the voices of well-known figures in the spiritual and psychodynamic fields. Bizarre, exclusive, esoteric teaching did not figure in the discourse, even if such bold speculations as transcend mere human knowledge did illuminate the talk and the questions that followed from it.

The one observation that flowed out of the whole discussion was the unitary nature of the human being: body, mind (the reasoning faculty), soul (the feeling, evaluating aspect) and spirit (the centre of thrusting onward growth animated by the Spirit of God) are integrated into a whole person. Therefore healing that is real cannot bypass any of these four functions of human personality. The healing I was subsequently to experience in Brighton at the hands of Constance Peters, while emphasizing the bodily aspect of personality, was to enrich the immaterial aspects of mind, soul and spirit also. My subsequent connexion with Mary's education centre was to acquaint me more intimately with her mode of thought and that of the people around her. As I learned more, so I was able to see the deficiency as well as the strength in what she believed and taught. By contrast, Constance's teaching had a traditional biblical basis with a strong flavouring of positive thinking. She would not countenance the negative thought that any of her circle might not recover completely after an illness or surgical operation. As her experience broadened, so did her patronage of spiritual literature become more eclectic and her dependence on church support grow less. One must object, however, that an obvious weakness of positive thinking preached as an essential prerequisite for healing work is that on some occasions healing does not occur, despite devout prayer and exemplary optimism in the face of adversity. We cannot manipulate the Holy Spirit, the primary agent of all healing, whether spiritual or medical, to suit ourselves. Indeed, we have instead to be available to be used by God for ventures so precarious in essence that only his grace can see us through the void of darkness. In a rather similar way, Mary's approach was flawed by her own special type of dogmatism that often could

9

not tolerate any opposition no matter how constructive it tried to be. Clinging is the particular vice of us here on earth; slowly indeed do we learn the lesson of renunciation, usually only when retirement enfolds us and death beckons us to its unknown realms.

My third experience of healing concerned Ronald Beesley, a powerful psychic healer who also taught a holistic type of philosophy with strongly esoteric overtones. I had first met him at a conference, and his psychic gifts impressed me at once. He asked me directly when I would commence the work I had been called to do, to wake up and declare myself fully for the destiny in front of me. This happened slightly earlier than the first healing episode I have described, and while I was in the midst of my involvement with Mary's education centre. I spent two weeks at his delightful 'centre' in the country in the early spring of 1963. At this time my professional work was in serious jeopardy because of the malice of a senior colleague who had power over my future career. I surrendered everything to God, and in the centre I met about twelve people, of various undistinguished backgrounds, engaged in a similar search for wholeness. If I had been unco-operative in the healing service at Brighton until the very last moment, here I was all agog, almost to the extent of suggestibility. I was later amazed how easily I had surrendered my critical faculties in a desire for inner enlightenment and outer healing. The course itself was memorable for the beauty of the late March and early April countryside no less than for the warmth and openness of Ronald, his assistants, and my fellow-students. We were regaled with an esoteric view of the nature of the human personality that owed much to Hindu and various theosophical insights. Ronald had only modest educational attainments, due to the poverty of his background, but he was an inspirational speaker of such conviction that to question any of his statements would have seemed well-nigh sacrilegious. In fact, the burden of what he said had an inner ring of truth apart from basic common sense.

He claimed to have a deeper knowledge of each of us – a property common to mediums generally, and he was in fact a medium of intense potency. And yet when I pondered over his character delineations both of me personally and the others generally, I could not fail to see how pretentiously imprecise they really were. In a state of suggestibility, especially when this is consciously induced, one can be talked into believing anything. Ronald did indeed have a fine pair of hands that could both heal and manipulate on the much-used orthopaedic couch, but on this occasion no startling organic cures showed themselves among us. He did seem to effect a slight raising of the fallen arches of my feet which was then sustained by the rather uncomfortable arch supports he provided, but in fact the effect was only small, and it was later to be reversed so much that the final condition has been, if anything, worse than the original. One has, however, with due respect to remember that dropped arches and other ortho-paedic deformities do tend to deteriorate with the ageing process. We were all, in fact, treated to a psychic display with esoteric overtones of great potency, but few of us came away manifestly healed of any infirmities that might have afflicted us beforehand.

The strength of that fortnight, using the hindsight that has accrued over many years' experience in the healing field, was one of establishing a creative relationship with the teacher and one's fellow-students. Relationships are the very basis of healing, inasmuch as the Holy Spirit works between soul and soul through the universal Spirit shared by all souls. I had in that fortnight been given my marching orders with the blessing of that far from orthodox teacher, and in September of the same year was to establish my own 'centre' in a humble room in a rather unattractive part of London. I had made a vow to God that I would never charge for my services, and so I could not afford anything more capacious at that time. As is so often the case, my financial position gradually improved sufficiently for me to work in more adequate quarters, but I shall never forget my early period of practice when I learned that what I had to give flowed from my depths in attentive conversation with those who had come to visit me. The laying-on of hands, performed in a stillness of rapt prayer, was the zenith of the session but not necessarily more important than the period of counselling that had preceded it.

As regards the gifted man himself who had, as it were, initiated me into the ministry of healing, Ronald was somewhat embittered. His amazing psychic gifts were spurned by the Church, who had few qualms in identifying them with demonic powers. The medical profession had no use for unorthodox methods of healing – today its approach is more open, but its conclusions are still heavily prejudiced against the validity of any method that cannot be accounted for in terms of reason. This 'reason' is synonymous with the logic-chopping function of the mind rather than the enlightened outpouring of the soul in direct communication with sources of inspiration beyond human understanding. The origin of these sources is the Spirit of God, the 'pneuma' of New Testament writers, especially St Paul. It is also identified with the enlightened mind, the 'nous' of the Wisdom tradition of the Bible, which is seen by St John to be manifested in the flesh by Jesus himself (John 6:35 and 7:38 are symbolic texts that illuminate the Wisdom of God as incarnated in Jesus). The point of the matter is that spiritual healing cannot be neatly reduced to rational categories summarily analysed by the discursive mind. Instead, the healing wrought by the Spirit broadens the mind and opens to its gaze immense vistas of potentiality foreign to the purely material agencies of education that necessarily dominate our secular environment.

Indeed, we are obliged to work under the limitations and control of the body while in this world, a world of heavy, often inert matter, yet holy at the same time. In other words the earth contains its own validity, and the Spirit of God incarnates perpetually in order to raise it up from torpid inertia to radiant life that finds its end in a transfiguration of shattering vibrancy calling the very dead to renewed life. The limitation of the healer I have described was his hostile attitude to the medical profession and the Church – understandable as this was, considering their insensitive attitude to him. But in the end we have to move beyond prejudice, both our own and that of others directed against us, so as to embrace the full gamut of God's providential care for us. In the end

12

we cannot evade the spiritual issues of life, and these are most carefully preserved and guarded by the various religious traditions that have come down to us. Polluted as they so often have been by venal, power-seeking professional agents, they still preserve the essence of faith that has been revealed in the lives of the saints of the tradition. It is indeed their witness that has kept the tradition alive when everything was falling to pieces around it. But at the same time the material agencies have their own validity, and are spurned only to our own cost.

The essence of healing is catholicity, an all-embracing sympathy that rejects nothing of help wherever it may come. This is the true holism that is so widely canvassed at the present time, yet so often repudiated by its very exponents in their personal prejudices against any factor they do not like to consider in the search for truth. There is no other field of human endeavour that lays bare one's inner nature with all its weaknesses so clearly as the healing ministry. But it is also an endeavour that fulfils the innate nobility of human nature as it aspires painfully to the vision of God.

2

The Call to Heal

No one can enter the field of healing, either as practitioner or as patient, without his inner nature being remorselessly laid bare. He is entering a field of the closest type of relationship: God is the centre and the people involved are the periphery, the circumference of the circle. Each is essential for the working of the whole. The energizing power is provided by the Spirit of God, who is the Life-giver as well as the One who shows the way. The way is a purgation of such an intensity that each person is brought to a confrontation of the essence of God within himself. The spark of the divine is both the source of encouragement in times of doubt and the measure of judgement during excesses of self-adulation, when one really believes one has the answer to the engima of life or that God is wholly on one's side. And so we are buffeted by an encouragement that keeps us moving and a restraint that stills us in its severity. God desires the whole person for himself, the blemishes so healed that the chastened heart can with confidence present itself to its Maker.

Why does a person become involved in the healing ministry? There is only one answer that is authentic: he or she has been called to it, just as Jeremiah was called to the prophetic ministry even at the time of his conception. The obedience to God cost him very dearly, almost his life on several occasions, but he could not stand back. In the story of Jonah the attempts of the prophet to evade his duty are ludicrously foiled by God, who looks down at the antics of his servant with amused patience and good-humoured tolerance. Had Jonah actually had the effrontery to reject the divine call categorically, he would have died, since he would have shut off the inflow of the Holy Spirit on whom all life depends. In fact, one can as easily close one's soul to that divine command as one's lungs to the need of air. The tension mounts rapidly to such a pitch that repentance is inevitable. This, incidentally, is the answer to those who believe that they have not heard the divine injunction and fear that their lives are being wasted in the wrong type of work. When the call comes, it is so clear that it cannot be mistaken. Even if, as in the instance of Jeremiah, the summons is one of dedication to the point of ceaseless pain, it none the less causes the heart to leap to attention with a joy that overrides any personal reservations.

The call to heal is from God. It is his will, we may be sure, that every person should be healed, since God's nature is love. But the divine way of healing far transcends our own limited understanding. We look for an immediate cure, whereas God requires no less than a complete change of perspective, a metanoia, in fact, so that the individual may perform his apportioned task properly, while at the same time growing into the stature of the complete person shown definitively in the lives of the world's saints; in the Christian tradition Jesus would be the model as well as the destination. Therefore our life on earth is an adventure. We are essentially strangers here, for our true home is in the heaven of mutual recognition and sharing, where we can be fully ourselves in the presence of the One whose radiance infuses all things, bringing them immortality. The way is hard and solitary; each of us marks out his or her own tracks, for no two lives can ever be identical in their journey, even if they share a common destination. And so to feel called to heal contains within the summons an arrogance that has to be faced and surmounted, and a trepidation that is to be accepted and yielded to God, as did the prophets of Israel. Usually it is the arrogance that predominates in many healers; time, however, disabuses them of many childish preconceptions.

Though the call is divine, the mouthpiece of God is usually

another person firmly established in a healing ministry. It is less common for the person to know intuitively that he or she has a healing gift. In my own case, I was aware of such a possibility, but it needed the ministry of the friends I have already mentioned to bring the gift to the surface so that I had the confidence as well as the self-criticism to commence the work. After the send-off the work is slow and lonely. Of the three friends, one did offer to support me, but in fact he was so immersed in his own activities that he probably forgot his offer: in the end this was rather fortunate, because my approach was dissimilar to his, due as much to differences in personality as to theology and background training. How I longed to possess his psychic powers, until I began to see how intrusive they could be! Not only are such gifts unreliable, no matter how assured the practitioner may be, but they almost inevitably lead to an unwelcome invasion of the client's inner sanctuary of peace and a superior attitude of judgement over that person. Jesus had such powers of inner vision – it was claimed of him that he knew men so well that he needed no evidence from others about a person, for he himself could tell what was in a man (John 2:25). But the difference between a truly spiritual intuition and a merely psychic intrusion is that the former is authoritative and benign, whereas the latter is coloured by the invader's prejudices and is potentially harmful to the person whose psyche has been invaded. Admittedly, in the ministry of deliverance, intimations of the inner disposition of afflicted people may be vouchsafed one, but they are fleeting and only immediately useful for the cleansing work at hand.

Here indeed we come squarely against a temptation that lies ahead of all those who feel called to the healing ministry: the lust for power with its corresponding desire for recognition. Many people enter the paranormal fields of adventure because they are dissatisfied with the crude materialism of the world around them. This dissatisfaction may stem from a variety of sources. Many seekers have personality problems that burden them with a feeling of inferiority. Their showing in the world of affairs may have been less impressive than might have been wished. The lack of the recognition they feel is their due may have led them to more obscure fields of endeavour where they can attain a more 'occult' type of knowledge with the power promised by skilled practitioners in that field. To claim healing powers is certainly an attractive prize as much for the boost it affords a cowering personality as for any material recompense. One becomes a member of a self-styled élite, a gnostic sect who can disdain the beliefs of ordinary people, to say nothing of the dogmas of orthodox religion. When one knows the hidden meaning of the Scriptures and sees the plan of life in all its glory, one – not unnaturally – feels decidedly superior. The superiority may appear to be related to society generally, but it is at heart an escape from the memory of the previous impotence of the seeker when he functioned as an inconsequential worm in a world of material values where affluence was the criterion of success. Such an individual may be approached by the leader of the group and told he has healing powers. Alternatively the message may come through a medium in the course of a spiritualistic seance or less spectacularly during casual conversation. At any rate, his ego has been boosted, and though his state of inner health is appalling, he is intent on nothing less than bringing healing to others! Well does Christ enjoin us to remove the plank from our own eye before we proceed to take the speck out of the eyes of those around us (Matthew 7:5)! In fact, this clearance of vision is a life-long process; if we were to wait for perfect sight, we would never be fit to help anyone else. As we strive to be of assistance in the humility of graciousness, so our vision, both physical and spiritual, does tend to strengthen. But we have to learn to call on the name of the Lord first, and not depend on any man-made contrivances, to say nothing of the indeterminate agencies liable to inhabit the psychic field.

Another, far more reputable, entrance to the healing field is through the Church's ministry. The healing ministry, so vital to the work of Jesus and of his disciples during the events described in the Acts of the Apostles, seems to have gradually dropped out of fashion as the power of the Christian Church waxed in political strength allied to military force. But a witness of healing was preserved even if it had to flourish underground. It has even been argued that the miraculous healing powers of Jesus and his immediate circle were a special dispensation of God, and not to be relied on, let alone cultivated, subsequently. Healing was to be of a more rational nature, associated with the scientific method and requiring the discipline of the human mind: the end was to be modern medical practice, whose advances, even in our own short time of witness, have been truly breathtaking. 'Dispensationalism' is no longer accepted as a part of orthodox doctrine, but its insight should not be dismissed as pure heresy: we have to participate with our whole being in the never-ceasing creative acts of God in our small world. This is both our duty and our privilege. Although Jesus could perform the miracle of feeding the five thousand with bread and fish (an episode recounted in all four Gospels, as if to emphasize its special importance), St Paul relied on the more usual way of collecting money from the various communities in the Diaspora to relieve the needs of the parent church in Jerusalem, especially after the prophet Agabus had forecast a severe famine in the region (Acts 11:27–30).

In more recent times the healing ministry has come progressively into its own. Not only have gifted individuals like Constance Peters emerged, but the larger movement of Renewal, also called the Charismatic Movement, has manifested itself, often with dramatic insistence, in the mainstream Christian denominations. There can be no doubt that this Renewal has deepened the spiritual life of many previously nominal churchgoers, as its results have opened areas of awareness that had before been hidden. It seems as if the previous emotional and intellectual barriers of the person are broken down, so that the God who knocks so persistently at the tightly shut door of the soul can now be heeded and welcomed inside. The joy of recognition is great; the unintelligible, though very meaningful, language of 'tongues' (also called glossolalia) is a response of the soul to its newly acquired intimacy with God (as seen in the person of Christ). The barriers of fear, suspicion and intellectual arrogance are surmounted, and the Holy Spirit pours through the personality of believers so that they feel they have been born again into the faith that they inherited secondhand but have only now come to know and to own. Not only may there be a dramatic inner healing of the person's psyche but the power of God may also effect amazing changes in the outer vesture, which is the physical body. Such, at any rate, would be the theory underlying the experience of Renewal, both personal and communal, and there is much truth in it.

A meeting of Renewal has elements strangely reminiscent of those encountered in frankly psychic groups. The Spirit flows through the meeting, imparting to various members important individual directives, while a 'word of knowledge' issuing from the mouth of someone present may seem to be directed quite deliberately to the condition of another member of the group. Not infrequently a member may be specifically commissioned for a particular ministry in the Church; healing is one such example, though often a large group would be engaged in the work. The 'word of knowledge', like the instruction given by a medium in a spiritualistic meeting, is itself open to question. Is it really an instruction from the Holy Spirit (or a discarnate source in the case of a spiritualistic seance) or merely the opinion of the speaker directed to the person already known to him (or her)? Discernment alone can furnish the answer; my own view tends naturally to scepticism, but on occasions it seems as if a genuine stranger does indeed receive a message remarkably pertinent to his or her situation and helpful for its progress. More usually the communication is of such a general quality that it can apply equally to a great number of people with difficulties or perplexities about their future actions.

There can, however, be no doubt that the Pentecostal churches and their counterparts in the mainstream Christian tradition, both Catholic and Reformed, have renewed the strength of the healing ministry and brought to the fore a number of celebrated ministers of healing – a term I prefer to 'healer', which lays too much stress on the individual's gift. If esoteric teaching tends to make its practitioners feel rather a cut above the general run of humanity so that they can look down with pity on the ignorance of the masses, including the devout churchgoers, the Renewal Movement can hardly avoid inflating its adherents with a conviction of infallibility inasmuch as the Holy Spirit himself is their inspirer and guide. As St Paul would put it, 'If God is on our side, who is against us?' (Romans 8:31). The deduction is therefore only too easy that those who do healing work under non-Christian auspices – and especially those with spiritualistic affinities – are allied to the powers of darkness which produce immediate relief only to draw their victims more inextricably into their grasp prior to their final destruction. The fact that phenomena typical of Renewal can also be encountered in non-Christian esoteric circles is attributed to the mimicking powers of the devil, who can impersonate the angels of light so convincingly as to deceive the very elect.

Can the desire to heal have a dark undertone? Certainly there have been, and are, people with a conspicuous healing gift whose personal character has been far from wholesome. The notorious Russian healer Rasputin gained control over the royal household to the extent that the government of the country was under his malign spell; his assassination by two highly placed aristocrats sparked off the Russian Revolution that saw the murder of the royal family and the implementation of a communist dictatorship that has constantly persecuted all forms of worship up to the present day. On a less dramatic level there have been healers who have so controlled the lives of their clients that they have been forced to sacrifice their power of personal judgement to the whim of their despotic helper. It would no doubt be comforting to the believer if one could place all such predatory healers in the esoteric, spiritualistic camp while exonerating all Christian Charismatic individuals from this tendency, but in fact there is no sharp line of demarcation between the two groups. Each has its dictatorial, despotic element that does much harm by threatening those it treats with dire retribution if they do not carry out the recommendations of the practitioner in question. It is only too clear that the minister of healing in both groups may be inspired with amazing faith while remaining distressingly immature as a human being. It has been asserted that the healing consequent on the Charismatic Renewal Movement is permanent, while the effect of the non-Christian camp is temporary and indeed often succeeded by even worse trouble, but this again is open to question. I have seen remarkable results stemming from both groups, and also disastrous failures. Much seems to depend on the gift of the practitioner and his inner sanctity; unfortunately, even Christian Charismatic groups have their dark residue. Jesus does well to remind us that not everyone who calls him 'Lord, Lord' will enter the Kingdom of heaven, but only those who do the will of his heavenly Father. Even such charismatic feats as prophecy, deliverance and miracle-working do not automatically receive the divine accolade even when performed in the name of Christ (Matthew 7:21–23).

It seems to me that God's will is love, inasmuch as God is love and our own love is contingent on his love for us. Therefore anyone who practises the ministry of healing in an attitude of love for the person he is treating is at least on the right path. The more he can surrender his own desires to the divine will, the more harmless he will be, and the more benefit will follow his ministrations. But if he nurses hatred in his heart, his work is almost certain to be undermined, no matter how impeccable his theology may appear. Members of Renewal groups hate the devil and all his works. Since they believe they are guided by the Holy Spirit, it follows, according to this reasoning, that any other avenue of spiritual healing is demonic. The criterion of acceptability soon narrows down to a dogmatic scriptural literalism, notwithstanding the wide range of religious experience described in the Bible and the progressive revelation of the nature of God that emerges as the pages unfold. The God of terrible wrath of the Genesis–Exodus period slowly broadens to the God of benign justice of the Wisdom Books of the Old Testament and the loving God of many of the prophets (especially Hosea), Psalm 103, and finally much of the New Testament. Furthermore, as the nature of God's love unfolds, so does fear recede into the background: there is no room for fear in love; perfect love banishes fear (1 John 4:18).

The fear of the devil of many members of the Renewal Movement brings a dark shadow, a heavy sediment of hatred, into the depths of the group. This does not mean that we should have a liberal, permissive view that minimizes the terrible power of evil in the world. It simply reminds us that if we fight the enemy with his own weapons, we shall come to resemble him more and more. Jesus' advice about not setting ourselves against those who wrong us, and loving our enemies (Matthew 5:38–48) may seem visionary and other-worldly, but especially in healing matters it is remarkably practical. Our protector is God. In him alone is safety. This is a hard teaching to practise, for it stretches our faith almost to the point of breaking. But as soon as we take matters into our own hands, we assume the divine prerogative and the results are lethal: the various persecutions and inquisitions of the past are our warning lights, while the Holocaust and other atrocities of our own century show us the end of hatred. 'Justice is mine, says the Lord, I will repay' (Romans 12:19). St Paul goes on, in verse 21, to enjoin us not to let evil conquer us, but to use good to defeat evil. The good thing is love, not naked force, which has never won the final victory, since it always leaves a residue of hatred lurking in the back-ground, waiting patiently for its own time of revenge.

In my opinion the gifts of healing (whether by contact, counselling relationship, discernment of spirits, or simply an outflowing, affectionate temperament) are innate. Just as one person may have a natural aptitude for music or mathematics, for athletics or finance, for government or scientific research, so there are others who display some healing gift. As St Paul reminds us in 1 Corinthians 12:1–11, there are a number of spiritual gifts, and a single individual is unlikely to excel at them all (unless he, like Jesus, is a divine genius). Indeed, it is quite right that we should be deficient in some qualities, so that we may learn to receive in humility and not only bestow our gifts with a superior graciousness on our lesser brethren. These gifts, whether of healing or of more secular attainment, are morally neutral. They can be used for the public good or the individual's private gain.

The second way brings with it more immediate dividends, but in the end we find that the gift becomes a prison rather than an asset; we have to cling onto it at all costs since our very identity hinges on its display and the ensuing acclamation. Those who tread the 'occult', psychic path are in constant danger of the gift's dominating them and, like Frankenstein's monster, eventually encompassing their ruin. In addition, they are open to psychic assault by malign elements in the milieu in which they function – these elements may be both human and demonic. It is for this reason that I strongly discourage people from getting involved in spiritualistic circles and groups that explore the 'occult' dimension. The question is simple: 'Who is in command?' There can be only one proper answer, God himself, if the exploration is to be safe. But, in fact, it is the group leader or some psychic intermediary that dictates the work, which invariably comes to a sticky end, no matter how sincere the protestations of the participants may be. How easy it is to delude oneself with spiritual platitudes when the ego is simply looking for new fields to conquer! And yet natural psychic openness is not bad in itself. Without it our relationships would be barren intellectual forays, with a strong element of sensual stimulation thrown in, such as we witness among our animal companions.

I believe that one of the functions of the Renewal Movement in the Church was to elevate natural psychic gifts to spiritual excellence, with God in Christ as the true leader as well as the destination of our endeavours. Just as divine grace perfects nature, so that it starts to function as God would have it and not according to the aberrant working of selfish humanity, so do the natural gifts of God (for he is the Provider of all things in heaven and earth) acquire an added radiance when they are dedicated to him and, by extension, the whole of the created order. The two great commandments, to love God with our whole being and to love our neighbour as ourself, are thus affirmed, remembering that the love of God must precede all other proclaimed love if that love is real and not merely a clinging possessiveness. Once we know and can, in our own feeble way, reciprocate the love of God, we no longer need the support of our human brethren to substantiate our own identity. Then at last we can love them for themselves alone without looking for any response, let alone reward. Love, like virtue, is its own reward, and when it can be received in innocent trust, it brings with it a glorious healing radiance. This is the divine illumination that should infuse all human activity, whether physical, mental, emotional or psychic (remembering that the psychic field is closely linked to the emotions and rather more distantly to the reason).

Unfortunately that divine love is not always to be found in Renewal groups. As we have already noted, fear and hatred are sometimes distressingly evident, so that the fully renewing power of the Holy Spirit has not been allowed to cleanse and radiate the psychic faculty as well as it might. We cannot control the flow of God's Spirit, who blows where he wills and not only along those channels we have constructed for his passage. If we are not fully open in trust, the Holy Spirit cannot enter into our lives, and so we remain on the periphery of divine healing. In this way the movement of Renewal has often had a divisive effect on congregations and not the unifying one seen with a full working of the Holy Spirit – 'Spare no effort to make fast with bonds of peace the unity which the Spirit gives' (Ephesians 4:3).

It is indeed a venture of faith to enter the healing ministry. It is truly falling into the hands of the Living God. We may feel that we are especially gifted to have been called to heal, but first of all we have to be healed ourselves of all illusions as well as the many impurities that sully our private lives. There is one Holy Spirit who is the Author of healing as an integral part of his life-giving function. His inspiration plays on all those engaged in healing work, whatever their belief or personal integrity. Just as God makes his sun rise on good and bad alike and sends the rain on the honest and the dishonest (Matthew 5:45), so his Spirit is with us all in our work day by day. I have no doubt that all healing has a common source, but unfortunately the rays can be deflected and misdirected by sinful people. Whether a healing ministry is divine or demonic depends not so much on the professed beliefs of the practitioner as on the purity of his heart. The acid test is that of Jesus: you will recognize them by their fruits (Matthew 7:15–20). These are the fruits of the Spirit of which love, joy and peace are the first three – the others are patience, kindness, goodness, fidelity, gentleness and, last but

24

not least, self-control (Galatians 5:22). One's way into the ministry may seem, on later reflection, to have been decidedly suspect and one's early associates extremely eccentric, if not deluded, in their own belief systems. But one learns to plough one's own furrow as experience opens one's mind to new revelations of the Holy Spirit.

3

The Burden of Disclosure

One cannot enter fully into the healing ministry until one is so emptied of guile, so shriven of deceit, so cleansed of greed, that the Spirit of God may fill the void left inside one. When people tell me they feel called to this ministry – and I speak especially of those who have not received a direct intimation at an esoteric gathering or a Renewal group – I always ask them why they wish to be involved in healing. I remind them that the work is taxing and brings little reward: indeed, the very thought of reward tends to stultify the healing power. Most of these people believe they are called to relieve suffering and cure ill-health, but in fact there is frequently a strong drive to power or egoistical assertiveness behind the laudable, and usually quite sincere, desire to help others. This applies also to those who enter the healing field through spiritualistic agencies or the Renewal Movement.

In my experience, already described, I had the benefit of a triple introduction by a fairly mainstream Christian, a mystic with universalistic sympathies, and a psychically gifted esotericist. With hindsight I can see how mixed the motives were in all three of my revered mentors; in terms of integrity I could fault none of them. Their whole lives were dedicated, in accordance with their special gift and at great cost, to proclaiming the spiritual nature of human personality in the ears of a largely indifferent, if not hostile, public. But none of them had fully gained charge of the ego with its demands for personal recompense, at least until near the end of their lives, and so their unique work was clouded by persistent longings for personal recognition in a world of aloof professionals. Had they been able to display reputable diplomas and to disport learned academic connexions, it is probable that the course of the work might have been more auspicious, but in the end they would, like Jesus, at God's behest, have been obliged to forgo the support of material recognition and enter the wilderness of pitilessly cold isolation, there to be tempted to renounce their vision by the prince of this world whom we call Satan, or the devil. Indeed, this aspect of the work of the evil one is much more crafty and destructive than his far better publicized activities in the realm of deliverance. This aspect excites fear by virtue of ill-informed publicity as much as the threat of demonic assault.

In the instance of my three friends, there was no fear to stand up for their beliefs. They were not afraid to display their wares to the world, hoping for at least some response, but none of them was fully open to personal criticism or able to face the inadequate sides of their own teachings. How hard it is to tolerate dissension especially when one is a pioneer, the custodian of a new way of thought! I too became involved in a totally unorthodox way of healing – in respect of the medical profession, and therefore to the jeopardy of my professional reputation – as much through inner dereliction and selfish curiosity as a concern for people. I was well aware of the ambivalence in my attitude which allowed me to associate my name with these people, even speaking on their behalf in closed groups, yet not supporting them wholeheartedly in public. Years were to elapse before I could lose myself sufficiently to proclaim my spiritual creed in word and practice without deference to any mundane powers.

We have already considered Jesus' teaching about the need for clear sight before we can help other people. In fact, there are few more satisfying activities than meddling in other people's affairs, for not only does this avert our gaze from the disorder within but it also serves to boost the ego. Many self-styled healers have a conspicuously inflated ego, the use of which helps to put out of mind any inner problems that might

threaten their self-esteem. When the subterfuge is finally
exposed, they may collapse in the shock of self-discovery: all
that remains is a feeble, palpitating soul that has never been
allowed to reveal itself previously, to bear the impress of truth
that brings with it the renewing thrust of the Holy Spirit,
without whom life is impossible.

It follows that no one should enter the healing ministry
until they have the integrity to undertake a sober review of
their inner life. Without this awareness they are apt to project
their darkness onto other people, both on the level of the flesh
and in the depths of the soul. Of course, few of us are likely
to attain sanctity in this life. Not many attain great heights
of the spirit here on earth, and the most famous saints of the
Christian tradition (and no doubt other traditions also) have
protested their unworthiness even as they lay dying. This
protestation is no mere gesture of false modesty: we have all
failed in some way in the vocation of love to which we have
been called. It is that end to which Jesus urges his disciples
in his counsel of perfection that forms a peak of the Sermon
on the Mount (Matthew 5:48). To have attained that great
perfection is the end of all healing; just as the cells of the
body work in close support in a healthy organism, so do the
individual units of society function in unself-conscious service
to the benefit of the total population when they work from
an inner spring of love.

Unworthiness must not be confused with worthlessness. It
is questionable whether even the most noxious organism in
the realm of biology is totally devoid of some saving feature,
at least in the eyes of the Creator, even if we can find nothing
good in it. No human being is worthless, even if aeons have
to elapse before a person's destiny becomes apparent. I
believe that a divine intelligence governs all created forms,
and we, the most mentally advanced creatures in our little
world, have enormous potentiality lying dormant in the
depths of the soul. The essential function of the minister of
healing is to work with God in the liberation of his various
creatures from the restriction of disease. Then they may enter
the joy of a fulfilled life.

It is a strange, but important, paradox that earnest human

endeavour can, in some circumstances, actually impede the work of God. The spiritual life depends on grace, the unmerited gift of God, and the faith to accept it with the guilelessness of a child. Earnest human works, done with the best intentions, even to scale the ladder of perfection, may in the end cause the ladder to slip and fall with the aspirant caught between the rungs. We can, in other words, so easily get in the way of the very work we are commissioned to do that the power of the Holy Spirit is deflected from its purpose, if not temporarily annulled. And yet we read in Jeremiah 29:13: 'If you search with all your heart, I will let you find me, says the Lord.' The seeking, the endeavour, that leads to the vision of God and therefore to proper healing, must be a response of the whole person and not merely an aggressive ego. It is a strange observation by Jesus in Matthew 11:12, that since the coming of John the Baptist up to the present, the Kingdom of heaven has been subjected to violence and violent men are seizing it. The meaning of this saying is obscure, and so no definitive exegesis can be provided. It seems to me that violence can never be commended – at the most it may be unavoidable for defence when oneself or someone else, especially a defenceless child, is confronted by a violent assailant (wielding physical force, verbal abuse or moral seduction), and the attack should be called off at the earliest moment when law and order have been restored. If this is true in a merely personal context, how much more so is it in the way of spiritual life with its ascent in prayer to God! Those who try to force the portals of heaven open by their piety would tend to exclude all other seekers from its habitation. Their heaven would soon contract to a hell of narrow, self-centred conformity to a prevailing power who would seem to have closer affinities with the devil than with God. The history of dogmatic religion bears too many examples of this trend for our comfort; healing is certainly not a commodity of this sectarian heaven.

The doors of heaven are, in fact, open to all of us – we have simply to knock to be admitted. It is our own spiritual ill-health that impedes the journey, but the courtesy of God and his overflowing love do not change. The way is by contemplative prayer that finds its end in intercession for our fellow-creatures and the daily work of reconciliation that follows from it. In this way the works that heal the world stem from a faith in God and an openness to his love. As St James says, faith that does not lead to action is a lifeless thing (James 2:17), but action not based on faith (as St Paul might well retort), being self-centred, is very liable to end in disaster. The Tower of Babel story in Genesis 11:1–9 is a fine illustration of this theme, and it continues to be pursued by activist groups, including those involved in healing work, despite their genuine sincerity to do good. Their error is one of insolent pride (hubris). Nothing excludes the power of the Holy Spirit more surely than arrogance, a fault common even in Renewal groups, to say nothing of the esoteric contingent who pride themselves on their special source of knowledge. Religious triumphalism and esoteric 'gnosis' tend to impede God's action; humility is an essential precondition for its fulfilment in and through the practitioner.

And so should we simply be quiet and do nothing at all in order to serve God best? The answer has already been given: pray without ceasing and be attentive to the present moment. If you are aware now, you will be given the directive to future action and the power to perform it. There is in contemplative prayer a perfect coincidence of the divine and the human wills: God strengthens our natural faculties so that at last we can see what must be done, and do it accordingly. The final choice, however, is ours, since free will is the divine gift to us. All this stresses the importance of the reasoning function of the psyche, which we term the mind; on a technical level it is essential. The continued pre-eminence of the medical aspects of healing underlines this, and we should be grateful for them in their own place. But restricted medical knowledge may have such a circumscribed base that the practitioner is forced to confine himself to a narrow speciality, to the exclusion of a wider view of the healing process. In this respect allopathic medical practice (the orthodox medical approach) is an apparently ceaselessly expanding field of high-power technology. The developments in diagnostic techniques and surgical procedures over the past three decades have been so radical that the medical practice of the earlier part of this century seems almost medieval by contrast. This is excellent as far as it goes, but there still remain large areas of disease process as yet intractable to orthodox therapy. It seems almost as if the conquest of one disorder unmasks a new area of disease process; what was at one time rare or of only minor importance progressively unfolds into an urgent problem affecting considerable numbers of people. This is, paradoxically, a tribute to the advances in medical understanding: diseases that would frequently have killed a younger generation are now so well contained that the more unusual remnant has a less impeded opportunity to manifest itself. Furthermore, the increased longevity in the developed countries, a consequence of social improvement no less than medical advances, has led to the increased incidence of diseases found especially in the latter part of life.

The knowledge that brings us to God, the source of all healing, has to transcend the ego. In the action of humility required for this self-transcendence, the ego structure of the personality expands effortlessly until it coincides with a more comprehensive, deeper, internal principle of awareness, which is in fact the soul, or the true self. What does it profit a person if he wins the whole world at the cost of his true self (Mark 8:36)? In the consciousness of the soul, isolated knowledge of facts is encompassed in an awareness of over-all presence in whose radiance specialized worldly expertise is seen to constitute the mere foothills of the massive mountain of understanding and not its pinnacle. The over-all presence is revealed as a unitive knowledge of the person and God. Such a knowledge is all-embracing, and it broadens out to assume the character of wisdom. Wisdom pays due deference to specialized techniques and intellectual understanding, both of which are valid in their own context. But wisdom can integrate all disparate sources of knowledge into a whole that brings with it insights of meaning, purpose and destiny that lie beyond the capacity of the specialist agencies we know so well in our daily lives.

This unitive knowledge is the pattern of relationship that should prevail between the one giving, and the other receiving, healing. This applies especially to what is called spiritual healing (the laying-on of hands and prayer with anointing on special occasions), but ideally it should extend to counselling, psychotherapy and even orthodox medical practice. To many medical practitioners this demand would evoke astonishment as well as tolerant amusement; they officiate from a seat of authority, listening cursorily and prescribing summarily. The patient can all too easily assume the character of a mass of organs functioning in a physiological milieu of variable efficiency, and the object of treatment is to get the malfunction repaired as soon as possible, so that the milieu may be restored to a proper equilibrium. And so medical practice can frequently be regarded as high-grade technology. The doctor runs the risk of becoming essentially a technician rather than a person of wisdom and deeper concern for the one he or she treats. On the level of immediate cure this may seem quite acceptable, but unless there is a deeper understanding of the issues of ill-health, it is very likely that one malady will be succeeded by other even more unpleasant ones.

Empathy is at the very heart of healing work; as one's self-awareness enters into the personality of the individual one is treating, so one attains a sensitivity to his condition and can communicate fully with him. It is the crass insensitivity of some fervent religious groups that makes their witness offensive to many people. These groups tend to be judge-mental as they sit in self-imposed authority over the rest of the world. The gross insensitivity of some members of the medical profession is notorious. While we can with gratitude hail the great medical advances of our time, we cannot but regret the attrition of the doctor–patient relationship that all too often has accompanied them. The spectacular success of the profession may, paradoxically, become the basis of its future failure as an agency of healing, unless it learns to look inwards. But the Church itself often gives the impression of being more interested in distant political issues than in direct relationships with people.

On the whole, doctors tend to fight shy of metaphysical considerations such as their patients may broach, while many ministers of religion hide their own vulnerability under a convenient veil of platitudes culled from the Bible and various other spiritual writings. To the doctor success is equated with cure, whereas death is the supreme failure. This immature approach is typical of many healing agencies also: to the member of a Renewal group death might seem to deny God's victory over the forces of evil in the world, while the esotericist would have to acknowledge that his special source of power had proved ineffective. Behind this all too human approach to 'failure' lies the fear that challenges our self-assertiveness, the shrinking from the truth that we all display in times of trial, and the painful acceptance of our own frailty no matter what religious faith, esoteric knowledge, or technical skill we may parade to the world.

To have to descend to the helplessness of the person we are attempting to succour is the beginning of a truly healing relationship. No longer can we glibly pontificate from above; instead we have to learn in humility with the one who suffers. In a truly healing relationship we are, in other words, alongside the sufferer, not distant from him. We can in this respect hardly avert our gaze from the Christ who suffers the psychic hell of Gethsemane and the pain-racked humiliation of Calvary as he hangs crucified, as if in vigil, between two criminals. Before the Passion, Jesus is somewhat remote from others in his magisterial authority, whether over the demonic powers that influence the world or the voices of the religious teachers that promulgate the official spiritual doctrine. He is always in command; his disciples hang on his words while his adversaries retire discomfited. And then comes the final confrontation with evil: for once Jesus is silent, while his impotence under interrogation frightens his disciples into flight. He is now completely alone – as he always was in the depths of his soul – but now even the presence of his Father is blurred and indistinct. Well do the chief priests with the lawyers and elders mock him as he remains nailed to the cross: 'He saved others, but he cannot save himself. King of Israel, indeed! Let him come down now from the cross, and then we will believe him' (Matthew 27:42). Had he indeed shown his authority as they had challenged him to do, his

33

complete identification with the human condition would have been frustrated, and his healing work would have retained a certain distance which would have separated him from other people. At that moment he could heal by pure identification without the exercise of visible strength or spiritual authority. A new era of human relationship had begun: the Holy Spirit was now a living force binding people together in mutual recognition. The barriers of identity had been breached by a love that raised all creatures to a new level of potentiality. And yet the individual identity was confirmed and strengthened, not submerged in a sea of amorphous goodwill.

The minister of healing likewise stands alongside his client, and his vulnerability is the price of his healing power. It might be argued that if one were to take on the full burden of suffering of even a single person, let alone a number, in a healing-counselling session, the effect would be emotionally devastating and psychically depleting to the point of a complete physical breakdown. We can understand the medical practitioner standing aloof from the personality of a patient while concentrating with precision on the physical problem that has caused the sufferer to seek help: the emotional impact of so much suffering would become unbearable in even a short session together. In a situation of high technology such an approach becomes increasingly common, but the doctor–patient relationship is frayed almost to the point of severance. It is not surprising that, despite the manifest success of so much allopathic therapy, many patients are moving towards alternative fields of treatment. At least the practitioner has time available to speak to them as intelligent individuals and to enter into some of their personal problems. Dialogue has healing properties.

But the problem remains. How can one enter into the depths of a client's personality and yet remain unscathed? We remember in this respect Jesus feeling power being drained from himself by a woman with an embarrassing bleeding condition (probably from the womb) who touched him deliberately but without prior permission (Mark 5:25–34). Many lesser practitioners could relate similar incidents in the course of their work. Indeed, a very psychically

aware person can be drained by the atmosphere of a crowd
in a public place; even the congregation of a church has been
known to have a similar effect – but perhaps they picked up
something already present in the building. Churches are, in
my experience, seldom the best places for deep private prayer,
which is an indication of the poor quality of worship attained
in so many of them. The Reserved Sacrament can help to
lighten the atmosphere. T. S. Eliot, in *Little Gidding*, writes:

> You are not here to verify,
> Instruct yourself, or inform curiosity
> Or carry report. You are here to kneel
> Where prayer has been valid. And prayer is more
> Than an order of words, the conscious occupation
> Of the praying mind, or the sound of the voice praying.
> And what the dead had no speech for, when living,
> They can tell you, being dead: the communication
> Of the dead is tongued with fire beyond the language of the
> living.
> Here, the intersection of the timeless moment
> Is England and nowhere. Never and always.

Where prayer has been valid! This is the answer. The person
of prayer can enter the depths of another's woe with impunity
because he is close to God. In the divine presence all that is
morbid and unclean, disturbed and unhappy, is taken up,
healed and transfigured. One can then enter into the darkest
recesses of another person's psyche and act as a focus of light
in an atmosphere of dark tragedy, even despair. It seems that
Christ had this ability throughout his ministry. He formed so
close a psychic link with those who would receive his presence
that a healing power, the flow of the Holy Spirit, reached out
to them and healed them of their infirmities. If we could
attain the transparency of character in which the Holy Spirit
can flow without interference, we too would be effective ministers of healing. But what is first required is a radical cleansing
of the psyche, so that the light of God can illuminate even its
darkest recesses and fill the person with a healing radiance.

How can one recognize a true healing agent? By the radiance that flows from him. There is a transparency that shows
itself even to the naked eye, in the finest ministers of healing.

Somehow the native coarseness of the flesh is subtly transfigured, and the purity of the heart shines through the outer
vehicle, the physical body. We are reminded by St Paul that
our body is a shrine of the indwelling Holy Spirit, and the
Spirit is God's gift to us (1 Corinthians 6:19). He goes on to
remind us that we do not belong to ourselves, but that we
were bought for a price, and so we should honour God in our
body. When we reflect on the abuse of the body of mankind
by alcohol, smoking, drugs and sexual promiscuity that goes
on day after day, we can see how far we have departed from
the law that St Paul expounds. An effective minister of healing
should be able to control the desires of the flesh by the
indwelling Spirit. Admittedly there are some psychic healers,
such as Rasputin, who seem to combine profligacy with a gift
of contact healing, but their work is devoid of a spiritual base
and their clients do not grow as people. It is this type of
healing that brings the practice into disrepute among earnest
seekers after truth. It is for this reason that any native psychic
ability should be charged with the glory of God, so that it
shows itself as a spiritual power. By this I mean a power that
can transform the personality of the client into a sober, caring
presence.

The purgation of the personality is time-consuming; it is a
painful, humiliating process. Nothing can remain concealed
under the searing scrutiny of the Holy Spirit, but as the
revelation of the total personality proceeds, so there is a
remarkable sense of freedom. The eye of the soul is truly
relieved of the occluding plank, so that the Spirit of God can
shine through it to anyone outside who is in need. At the
same time it radiates inwards to heal the minister's own
bodily and mental problems. Indeed, one of the unseen, yet
very evident rewards of a truly spiritual healing ministry is a
progressive healing of the minister: as he gives, so does he
receive. The reward is not earthly riches but a spiritual
blessing.

It should finally be said that healing gifts are not equally
disposed among everybody. On the contrary, some people,
like the woman suffering from a bleeding condition mentioned
in the Gospel, are psychic depleters. I have met a number of

these who have been told by mediums that they have a healing gift. Perhaps the medium's 'guide' is speaking about the ultimate state of the person, but in the present dispensation such an individual is a liability, not an asset. In some Renewal groups each member of the meeting is instructed to lay hands on the one next to him, for the Holy Spirit is at work among them all. In one way this must be true, since he is the Life-giver, but it is open to doubt whether he operates in a special way among all the attenders of a Charismatic group. In my experience of such matters, some of those present do indeed seem to radiate a healing warmth in their touch, while others act to 'drain' their brethren. I do not favour the practice of group laying-on of hands even if the 'word of knowledge' comes from an apparently impeccable source. The same reservation applies even more strongly to psychic groups under instruction from the medium's guide (this is a personality that claims familiarity with the after-life situation; it is almost certainly a sub-personality of the medium, but may conceivably have a connexion with other realms of consciousness including the life beyond death). Our own common sense and power of discernment should never be allowed to be over-ridden by instructions coming from another person, however impressive the source may claim to be or what power it may seem to represent.

4

The Journey to Truth

Among the many people whom I see in a counselling and
healing capacity there was a minister of religion. He suffered
severely with digestive problems, so much so that a number
of surgical operations were necessary. He was also a member
of a Renewal group who prayed fervently for his recovery.
But when their own ministrations proved ineffective the group
grew increasingly restive. The afflicted one, a pastor indeed
and therefore especially close to God, was letting down the
group – and, by extension, God himself. Their obvious
impatience did not ease the poor man's indigestion. To his
physical pain the distress of guilt was added. The more he
tried to fulfil the expectations of the others, the worse did his
condition become. It was very evident that the members of
the group were as insecure emotionally as was their minister.
They looked for a God to prove himself by miracles in rather
the same way as Jesus' disciples did during the agony of his
betrayal and death. So much of the ministry of healing is
based on this premise: God wants us all to be healed of our
maladies, and if we are obedient enough in absolute faith and
righteous conduct he will cure us and bring us to health. In
fact, the faith and the conduct are part of the healing process.
God's grace is such that everyone who asks receives, but what
is obtained, in many situations, is not what was anticipated.
The very insistence of many healing groups that God should
show himself by fulfilling their requests to the letter often has

the effect of impeding the healing work of the Holy Spirit. God does not need to show his presence by miracles, events that cause us to marvel at the divine power by apparently transcending the usual course of nature.

Life itself is the supreme miracle, and the smooth running of so many of our routine activities day by day should be a cause for us to marvel, as it was for the writer of Psalm 139. If we are blind to the work of God in the course of health and prosperity, we are unlikely to appreciate divine intervention in times of trouble. Prayer is not primarily an urgent appeal to God to put right some present misfortune. It is first of all a tranquil, dedicated alignment of the human personality in humble service with the divine will, so that healing can flow to the world and the creative process can be quickened. It is the great privilege of the human to work with God in the unceasing creation of the world, a creation that, far from being complete and merely needing to be maintained, looks forward to the transmutation of material substance. All this is, needless to say, a remote teaching for a person afflicted in body or mind, longing only for release so as to enjoy something of the present delights of nature while there is yet time in his mortal life. But until a wider vision of life in eternity is attained, all present healing will be sadly transient. Indeed, a pagan view of life is tragic in its end, no matter how exquisite may be its immediate beauty. Spiritual intuition lifts this transient, fading beauty to the sphere of resurrection. The ministry of healing should be the outer manifestation of this resurrection of mortal forms to eternal presence. More usually, however, it is a glorified materialism that looks for a present cure to be pathetically nursed for as long as possible as a proof of God's power.

In the instance of the ailing pastor, failure attended the ministry of Renewal despite the fervent zeal and warm concern of all the group. The reason was not hard to find: he was being forced into a mould that was emphatically not his own. Indeed, the very intention of helping another person should be placed under critical scrutiny. While we can offer technical help with impunity – and this includes orthodox medical practice that has proved itself in the testing field of trial and error – we should tread warily into the lives of our fellow-creatures. Indeed, fools do often rush into a personal situation where angels would fear to tread. But a member of a Renewal group might produce a special 'word of knowledge' that could with authority claim entrance into another person's inner life, the very soul with its inviolate secret of identity. Since the word speaks with the authority of the Holy Spirit, it would take precedence over even the highest grade of the angelic hierarchy: it could tread with assurance and lead the afflicted person on the way to health. I found myself, on one occasion, in the company of someone who claimed a strong gift of 'sensitivity' (in this context, the alternative term for mediumship). She broached the question of my private life without any prior invitation, telling me of a message she had received concerning the way I should comport my affairs in the future. I was distinctly uneasy at what she had said, and was subsequently shown by the inner light of the soul quite clearly that she had made a precipitate, though well-intentioned, incursion into my private life, giving, in fact, a message that was heavily flavoured with her own opinions. I rebuked her subsequently, telling her that it was discourteous to intrude into the private affairs of another person, irrespective of any message given. If a prior request for guidance had been received, the matter would, of course, be different.

The point is that the external source giving the instruction, whatever claim may be made as to its identity and therefore its authority, is to be treated with reserve, and its validity challenged. If God does indeed have a special directive for us, he is very likely to speak to us personally and enlighten the soul without the need for intrusive outside assistance. If we are unsure of receiving and comprehending the inner directive, we are ill advised to accept it as a message from a masterful human source, which by its very nature is bound to colour the communication. Prophecy, even at its zenith as encountered in the Bible, cannot entirely escape this human contribution to the divine word. Therefore, the wise person, when presented with a message allegedly coming from the Holy Spirit, asks God for a direct confirmation rather than accepting it forthwith at its face value. Needless to say, the same caution is mandatory in respect of psychic and esoteric groups who practise healing. Here the danger of delusion is especially great.

In the case of my pastor friend, the basic problem was psychological, with spiritual overtones. He had spent his life trying to obey the rules laid down by the rather narrow religious tradition in which he had been reared. In the drama of his own life, he was having to bridge the enormous gulf between the complacent proclamation of traditional moral dogma that he delivered to his flock and the warm, yet cold and brutal, life of the streets around him. He had been imprisoned in a terrifying edifice of guilt, erected by himself even though the bricks were all aspects of the existence into which he had been thrust from the time of his birth. The healing group that had met to support him seemed regrettably only to have provided further building material for his prison in the shape of unremitting demands for faith and insinuations of unacknowledged sin when positive results had not been forthcoming.

The parallel between this by no means uncommon situation and the accusations of Job's comforters in response to his unrepentant cries of innocence and outrage strike home with immediate force. Job's very protestations of guiltlessness in the face of what appeared to be divine judgement convinced the three friends of his wrongfulness. True guilt does in fact interfere with faith, for the sense of deep underlying unworthiness serves to prevent the person from opening himself unreservedly to God's love. Guilt issues forth into the psyche like a sudden gust of heavy rainclouds that directly shut out the warm comfort of the sun's rays. The clouds of guilt stand in the way of the spirit of the soul, and the Holy Spirit, whose place of action is the human spirit, cannot infuse the personality of the afflicted person until there is a change of heart. And so the ministrations of the group, like those of Job's friends, exacerbated rather than relieved the situation by imposing a stigma of unworthiness upon him.

The healing work it was my privilege to do was to initiate the poor man's release from the bondage of past associations. Only then could his tortured psyche escape from the procrustean bed of the past into the liberating atmosphere of hope of the future. The laying-on of hands was sacramental of God's love as well as a means whereby the power of the Holy Spirit could penetrate to the depths of his receptive body, now opened by his liberated soul. The work continued for an extended period – indeed, it will never come to an end, for death merely closes a chapter in our living progress. The man himself in due course married and became the father of a small family. This previously inconceivable event served to strengthen his self-confidence, bringing a sense of authority into his life while opening new avenues of experience for him. The indigestion yielded remarkably in its intensity, but the tendency to stomach trouble persists and possibly always will. I believe we all have a special place of vulnerability in our bodies, our Achilles' heel as it were, which is especially liable to bear the brunt of life's vicissitudes. If we are wise we learn to live with our imperfect bodies, guarding them so that they in turn can serve us most efficiently for the particular work we are called to perform. Our innate frailty, by identifying us with the weakness of others, forms a point of departure for the adventure ahead of us, a life more fully used for the benefit of the world and our own increased satisfaction.

It is certain that we should view with distrust all instructions purporting to come from a high source that tend to invade another person's private life. Are all 'messages' therefore bad, or at any rate to be disregarded? Quite a number give encouragement, and these need not be summarily rejected: kindness from whatever source is at least immediately beneficial. But no message should be clung on to with obsessive devotion; at the most it is there to give the person hope during an especially difficult time of trial, and then it may be released. It has done its duty and so may depart in peace. Inasmuch as, in the thought of St Paul in Romans 8:18 and 28, the sufferings we now endure bear no comparison with the splendour, as yet unrevealed, which is in store for us, and all things work together for good for those who love God, we may travel ahead on our own apportioned path of self-actualization, knowing that there is a destination that will make every present travail a worthwhile experience. But we must have the faith to persist and the courage to continue the journey. It is in this context that inspirational messages can be of help.

Indeed, the ministry of healing finds its full flowering, its peak of endeavour, in this understanding of spiritual growth. Then it no longer dangles carrots of illusion in front of the sufferer (as occurs far too often in uninstructed groups who work with the best will in the world, but do great harm when their certainties fail to materialize), but it does promise unfailing support on the way. This is the ministry of faith, remembering that all of us progress by faith day by day. And then come sudden shafts of light that illuminate the way, so that we have the confidence to proceed onwards. The journey, though unique for each person, is a small part of a well-worn track trodden by humanity as a whole. St Paul emphasizes the love of God as a prerequisite for the working together for good of all the strange, often confusing events in our lives. While this love of God is a foundation for our healing journey, we grow increasingly into that love as we proceed on the way. This is because, as we grow in our own humanity, so are we able to accept the divine revelation more completely; the scales drop off our inner eyes, with the result that, whereas once we were inwardly blind, now we can see spiritually. As a consequence, our love of God grows stronger: we love because he loved us first (1 John 4:19).

In the healing process it is hardly to be wondered at that the patient looks for a rapid release from his sufferings. In other words, there is an unconscious self-concern, a true self-love, rather than any love for God. Self-love of this type is natural, but its motivation is not so much wrong-headed as inadequate. The second great commandment exhorts us to love our neighbour as ourself, and indeed, until we love ourselves sufficiently to take care of our bodies and relax our minds, we will never be able to love anyone else in a similar manner. But self-love is liable soon to become choked with personal desires if it is not guided and constantly inspired by a love that comes from God, and which is reciprocated by a warm, outflowing heart. And so, in the healing process, we should start by giving ourselves over to God's service in trust.

43

The ensuing peace that fills us allows the healing process time to repair our damaged bodies and minds. In the end we may be restored to something of the divine image in which we were created and which we have seen to best advantage in the saints of humanity, culminating in Christ himself. Then our service to our fellow-creatures will be immeasurably greater than before.

The contrast between precipitate selfish action and a dependence on God's love is starkly illustrated in the account of the Israelites' exodus from Egypt when they prepare to cross the Red Sea. This is symbolic of the last hurdle, and also the crucial one, in front of us all as we prepare to enter the full life of personal integrity, and so be more useful to those around us. When the Israelites are about to make the crossing, they are terrified at the sudden appearance of a large Egyptian force intent on their destruction. Indeed, they bewail their predicament and long for the slavery they so recently had escaped. But God, through his prophet Moses, tells them to stand firm and wait: he will do the necessary work. And as Moses stretches out his hand over the sea, the Lord drives away the waters to leave a dry sea-bed over which the multitude crosses with safety to the other side. When, however, Pharaoh's hosts pursue them, they can make no headway as their chariot wheels become clogged with sand. In terror they try to turn back, but then once again Moses stretches forth his hand under God's instruction, and the waters return to drown the retreating Egyptians. This fearsome account, an historic landmark in the Judaeo-Christian tradition but primitive in its understanding of God's love for all his creatures, teaches us that human activity ends in chaos and destruction unless it is informed by divine purpose. In the exodus saga it is evident that the Israelites, recalcitrant as they so frequently were, had a closer relationship with God than did their pagan neighbours. They therefore survived – and still survive – while their powerful persecutors fade into the mists of history. But they suffered – and still suffer – grievously for their periodic apostasies. God's end is a perfect humanity based on the image of Christ, and true healing cannot end until this goal has been attained.

Are bodily healings therefore to be denigrated? If this were the case, a major part of Jesus' ministry would be annulled. But the healing he bestowed so prodigally on all who came to him in faith was only the beginning of something far greater than anyone imagined. Perhaps Jesus' vision itself was somewhat restricted in this respect, for he was a full human being in the flesh and therefore subject to the limitation of knowledge that is our human lot. The primary and essential work of Jesus while he was alive on earth was to proclaim the Gospel of God: 'The time has come; the kingdom of God is upon you; repent, and believe the Gospel' (Mark 1:14–15). Jesus' healings (including the acts of deliverance) constituted a vital part of the Gospel, the Good News, and were tangible evidence of what that kingdom meant. It was a state of reparation of past damage and restoration of a fresh relationship with God, such as had existed at the beginning of the creation, described allegorically in the story of Adam and Eve. Just as these archetypal humans, in their self-centred way of life (which is the basis of sinfulness), were excluded from heaven, so the new humanity proclaimed and effected in the life of Christ was brought back once more. Heaven is a state of unitive relationship with God and therefore with the creation also.

In such a relationship the demands of the individual are fulfilled in the exaltation of the whole of creation. We are, in other words, most fully ourselves when we work in effortless freedom with our fellow-creatures, a freedom based on the service of God whose very nature is love. The more one strives for oneself, the more does one distance oneself from others as one's private affairs dominate one's life. The more circumscribed does one's identity become, the more isolated is one's existence. When, on the contrary, we work for the common good, our identity expands until such love infuses our life that we are in corporate unity with all things. This is heaven, and Christ's healings were signs of it: though they did not deserve any special consideration, ordinary sinful people were cured of impediments that had been spoiling their happiness, and no outer demand was made of them. The change was to be an inner one: that, as experience teaches us all, is disturbingly

45

slow and liable to relapse, because our own will is now engaged, and God does not, in his courtesy, interfere with the freedom of choice with which he has endowed us.

When all is going well for us, our faith is triumphant, but it tends to wane disastrously when shadows cross our path. It is then that we come to a deeper self-knowledge. This is the way of Christian discipleship and also a terse summary of the process of healing; it may start corporeally, in the body, but its end embraces the whole person, finally the body of humanity and with it the entire created order. A number of Jesus' healings illustrate this slow process. In one instance he cured ten men of a skin affliction termed leprosy (the exact nature of the disease remains obscure). Nine, all Jews and therefore sons of the covenant, did not so much as return to give thanks to Jesus and to praise God. Only one of the ten did this, and he was a Samaritan and therefore beyond the pale of respectable society (Luke 17:12–19). The nine ungrateful ones had hardly registered the miracle of their healing, so obtuse was their understanding. Only the outsider was truly on the healing path, though we may be sure that much had yet to be expunged from his character before even he could know the healing Christ.

On another occasion Jesus directly confronts a cripple of thirty-eight years' duration and asks him whether he really wants to be healed. He clearly divines an ambivalence in the man's attitude. The cripple tells Jesus that he is unable to enter the healing waters of the Sheep Pool in time, but it may well be that his hesitation is there to allow someone else to claim his place. His crippled condition certainly shields him from responsibilities that confront healthy people in the running of their lives. The man makes the decision for health, and Jesus at once cures him. But it is noteworthy that, when Jesus meets him later on, he impresses on the man the need for leaving behind sinful ways, or something even worse may afflict him. It is also of interest that, because the man, on Jesus' instruction, takes up his bed and is seen carrying it on the Sabbath, he is at once assailed for contravening the religious law. A new intensity has been infused into a previously sluggish existence. A spiritual responsibility has

46

been assumed, and it will not pass until all its requirements have been met (John 5:1–15).

The most impressive example in the Gospel, however, of slow, progressive healing, is that of the apostle Peter. He was closest to Jesus, at least in matters of everyday organization, and he was to assume leadership after the death of Christ. Yet he showed himself obtuse and cowardly when his Master was betrayed; it was his own skin that concerned him, to the extent that he denied any knowledge of the Lord and ran away to safety. Peter's initial healing coincided with Jesus' resurrection from the dead and the loving forgiveness bestowed on him as a weak but devoted disciple. After the Pentecostal experience of the outpouring of the Holy Spirit upon the disciples, Peter was the chief spokesman of the infant Christian community and was instrumental in bringing the first gentile convert Cornelius into its body. But he still liked to curry favour with the Jewish faction, and so he held back from eating with the gentile group when he was confronted with staunch Jewish Christians. St Paul opposed him to his face for his dishonesty (Galatians 2:11–14). It clearly took a long time before the apostle could become a person of sufficient integrity to give up his life for the truth, as his Master had done before him. Indeed, it is most important that we stay alive in the world until we have something worthwhile to give to God and, by implication, to our neighbours also. This is the measure of a true healing.

It seems that unpleasant experiences are still necessary for us to come to the ground of our own being. When things go well for us, our attention is focused on distant worldly objectives, not in any way to be deprecated in themselves so long as they do not blur our inner vision. In Jesus' terrible, rhetorical question already quoted: what good does it do a person if he gains the whole world at the cost of his inner integrity? Worldly success attained at the cost of our inner being, our soul or true self, has its own reward. In due course it recedes from us as disease and ageing ravage the body, and finally death closes the scene. What then do we have left as we make the shrouded journey to the after-life? This type of topic is not unnaturally embarrassing in worldly company, and indeed it

47

can easily become morbid, the preserve especially of the less materially successful type of person who looks for later rewards to redress the balance of an unsatisfactory life on earth. Nevertheless, the dark points of our life do give us time to consider the deeper aspects of reality. These can never be dismissed, for they grow in intensity as we prepare a balance sheet of our credits and debits prior to taking leave of this part of our existence. It is indeed a judgement against the superficial awareness of so many of us as we pursue the daily round of activity, that only a sharp reverse in fortune can bring us down to earth – and therefore to heaven also in the company of the One whose incarnation brought these two polarities into juxtaposition. Only when we have surmounted the test of faith and emerged victorious, if battered, can we begin to appreciate the present circumstances of a life that had previously been taken for granted.

Once adversity hits us we squeal in terror like our humbler animal brethren. We want relief as soon as possible, and the healing work of Christ is here to show us the unmerited love that God has for us all. But we too have to play our part: we must assimilate both the misfortune and the vision of divine reality that has been given us. This means declaring ourselves as workers for the Kingdom. This Kingdom is indeed not primarily of this world at all, but as we grow into it, it impinges on the work of society, so that finally all creation may be embraced in its welcoming love.

5

The Contribution of Faith

The essence of healing is an openness of the person to the flow of life within him. This life, the gift of the Holy Spirit, is the means whereby damaged tissues are repaired and noxious outside influences neutralized and eliminated. The surgeon may suture the wound, but it is the internal constitution of the patient that ensures that a healthy bridge of living tissue fills the breach permanently. The more we investigate the scientific basis of healing of diseased tissues, the more awe-inspiring is the intricacy of the process, and the more truly miraculous does the natural order show itself. Without faith, in the context of a trusting availability to the demands of the present moment, there is a failure to progress. The stagnation of life in a sentient creature finds its end in death. But if faith is restored in time, life flows into the inert organism and growth proceeds.

Jesus, in many of the healing miracles described in the Gospel, states that it was the afflicted person's faith that made him whole, that delivered him from his present incubus. But what is the full measure of that faith? Is it simply a blind optimism that all will be well in the end? If this were the case the final destination would be a hospital ward crammed with the sick and the dying. Indeed, on the level of earthly expectation, this is our common end – provided we are not killed prematurely in accidents or as victims of violence. But there are various degrees of inner preparation for the final scene of

49

the drama of an earthly life. It is here that faith plays its special part. In the Gospel, the words of Mary, when the archangel Gabriel announces to her the conception of Jesus, are fundamental: 'I am the Lord's servant; as you have spoken, so be it' (Luke 1:38). This is a trusting relationship with life, a confidence in the will and the ability of God to protect all those who have their being in him ('in him we live and move and have our existence', Acts 17:28). This relationship may be a directly personal one with the source of all life whom we call God, or else it may be an indirect, circumscribed one with one of his ministers. In this case, however, the faith must transcend the personality of the servant to attain knowledge of the source. In other words, faith finds its completion in silent acceptance of the divine power that creates the universe unceasingly, not merely alone, but in deference to the creatures' contributions that vary in nature according to their ability to respond, think and love. Faith in a person alone is very liable to degenerate into infatuation, emotional dependence, and eventually a renunciation of responsibility and will. The agent assumes the nature and function of a private god, and can in turn exert the power of a despot. This is especially liable to happen to those who traffic in the occult scene or who turn to mediums for guidance in the management of their intimate affairs.

The term 'faith healer' never fails to arouse intense hostility in me. It seems to contain, in the mind of the person who uses it, a suggestion that the minister of healing exerts a powerful psychic (or emotional) pressure (or attraction) on the personality of the one he tends, so that he demands absolute obedience and claims complete authority over the life of the sufferer. In other words, there has to be absolute trust in the agent, who assumes a masterfully directive role. And yet behind the façade of this imposing assertion of power there is a pervading, distinctly unpleasant aura of charlatanry, an esoteric jargon as well as an impressive display of personal magnetism. In the depths, however, there is nothing of any substance. The entire healing scene, and especially its esoteric faction, is pervaded by this scarcely definable yet distinctly unpleasant aroma of illusion. It is often emanated by the disturbed personalities of those who dominate that world and attain personal power and satisfaction through it. Indeed, they, like the crowd around Jesus' cross, do not know what they are doing. They can as easily destroy as create, raze to the ground as lift up to heaven. They are driven by a force from without that soon harnesses the vital energy within: evil lies close to goodness in the healing world.

It would seem impossible that the healing ministry could have a dark shadow side as well as the radiant warmth of love. But we have to face a universal law that the completely harmless is also certain to be completely ineffective. It is indeed a fearful thing to fall into the hands of the living God, for in his presence nothing can remain concealed any longer. In the same frame of reference we recall that Jesus, the Prince of Peace, does not come simply to bring peace on its own, but first of all a sword (Matthew 10:34). The same consideration of motivation and integrity applies with equal force to those who work within the ambit of the mainstream Christian tradition; their profession of belief is no guarantee of their motivation or even the sanctity of their ministry. We remember once more Jesus' caustic rejection of those who acclaim him but do not perform the Father's will even if they display remarkable charismatic gifts (Matthew 7:21–23). The operative word here is 'will': is it God's will or merely the uncleansed human will that is the directing force?

The Antichrist, the power of negation that works towards the annulment of God's creative work by the submergence of the whole cosmos into the darkness of chaos, may well display a benign, if not benevolent, face. I could easily imagine him dispensing bodily healings with profligate abandon to a large assembly of people even in a place of worship, so that the blind could see again, the deaf hear, the lame dance up and down the aisles with joy, and the near-dead rise up to new life to view the present spectacle with a vivid interest. And then he would say, like Jesus himself to the disciples after the resurrection event, 'Follow me'. Christ leads us to the abundant life of true relationship with ourselves, our neighbour and with God. The Antichrist betrays human relationships, corrupts truth and sullies beauty until his final end has been attained: annihilation into non-existence. The Christ, by contrast, raises up all created forms from the separate identity of the individual to the corporate union of the whole whose source and end is God. In the work of resurrection the ego self that is sacrificed is raised up into the true self that contains within it the spark of God. It is evident that a blind faith in the ministry of a healer can as easily lead to destruction as to wholeness. And, as we have already seen, the religious affiliation of the minister is no guarantee of his soundness.

How then can one discern an unsound healing agent from one that is reliable? We remember in this respect that all healing and power have their original source in God. His Holy Spirit infuses all beings with existence and life. The statement of Jesus to Pilate is extremely relevant here: when Pilate affirms the authority he has to release or to crucify Jesus, he is told by Jesus that he would have no authority over him if it had not been granted from above, and therefore the deeper guilt lies with the ones who handed Jesus over to him (John 19:11). In other words, they had used the power of God quite deliberately to perpetrate a murder, using Pilate's civic authority as their weapon. The power of the Holy Spirit both builds up and casts down. The demonic elements in creation, whose origin is shrouded in mystery but whose existence is ultimately under divine control inasmuch as God is the one supreme Creator of all cosmic forms and powers, are as much infused with the one power as are the agents of healing, reconciliation and light. It may well be that what we quite rightly call evil also has its part to play in the creative process; without it a drowsy complacency might tend to envelop the creature, so that it ventured no movement to spiritual awareness. This could be the way of spiritual evolution; unlike animal evolution, the will of the creature is involved in a free choice. Such an approach at least views evil not as something to be destroyed so much as to be converted and 'saved' in the context of being brought into a healing relationship with eternal life. But here silence is more eloquent than discourse: we learn by experience rather than by argument. Whatever may be the answer, it seems that an extended process in time is needed before the creature may know the all-embracing love of eternity. This is the experience of the personal love of God infused into the whole body of creation which now functions as a coherent totality. Evil is shown in divisiveness, whereas the good binds everything together in a union of mutual regard whose essential quality is love.

We should have no truck with evil – on this no morally aware person would disagree. But the question is how best to deal with it. Our very attempts to overcome it may let it attain mastery over us. Indeed, the world is a strange place, and life teaches us many unusual lessons. We have already seen how, in the peak of understanding, Jesus' teaching about non-resistance and co-operation with antagonistic agencies is the very basis of heaven. But for the challenge of evil forces, these final truths would remain hidden, since there would be no living thrust to evince them. But when they are brought out, a new generation of believers is born and a new world of enlightenment established.

It is no coincidence that God and Satan work hand-in-hand in the matter of Job's afflictions. Without these pains he would never have come to a mature self-knowledge (and also a critical appraisal of the traditional teaching that suffering is the inevitable fruit of sin, and a life of religious propriety has its certain worldly reward in prosperity and health). God sees to it that Job's life is preserved, but he does not interfere in any of the agony inflicted on him by the evil one. Only when Job has stood up to his adversity and refused to cower before the face of a traditionally all-powerful God of unquestioned righteousness, hoping thereby to attain a reprieve of his suffering, does God reveal himself directly to him. The experience is such that the shell of security under which Job had previously sheltered is shattered, and he can now confront the world with a confidence that does not depend on pious observances but on an overwhelming awareness of God's prodigal concern for every creature he has made. What he feared most did indeed befall him and without mitigation, but he emerged a person of a completely different stature to that of the wise philanthropist, a role he once so much valued. While in no way uninvolved in the world, he could now see his home in God and not in earthly matters. And so his new family relationships were more secure than the original ones, for there was no longer any clinging to people to provide strength and comfort. This is a hard way, the way in fact of bereavement, but the fruit is sustaining in a way that purely worldly rewards never can be. The fruit of bereavement is a growing intimacy with an ever-increasing number of people. Whereas worldly rewards come to an end, the deeper relationships of suffering fully mastered grow in extent as well as intensity far beyond the limits of this life.

Therefore, an unsound minister of healing is one whose own personality is so far from integration that he needs the assurance of positive results to strengthen his self-confidence. To be sure, he may be a member of a Renewal group and all glory may be given to Jesus, by whose Spirit the healings take place, but in fact it is the ego consciousness of the minister that is in charge and demands obedience. The same principle applies to those who work under a spiritualistic guide or the aegis of a group exploring the occult dimension. Such a person tends to demand absolute loyalty to himself no matter how impeccable the ultimate source may be regarded. The healer usually has scant regard for other healing agencies; medical practice especially is regarded as the dark rival, and every attempt is made to discredit its practitioners. Sometimes the client may be forbidden medical contact altogether.

A typical instance of this exclusiveness concerned a friend of mine with a slowly progressive, ultimately fatal, disease of the central nervous system called motor neurone disease. At one time it was called progressive muscular atrophy, and this is indeed how the condition manifests itself. There is a progressive wasting of the muscles of the upper and lower limbs so that the victim eventually becomes quite helpless. In due course the muscles of respiration also waste away, and the person succumbs to breathing problems. At present there is no effective treatment other than general measures to support the patient as efficiently as possible. It is hardly to be wondered at that the victims seek desperately for alternative means of allaying the relentless progress of their malady.

My friend fell into the hands of a medium who forecast

recovery provided she did not seek medical treatment. At the same time someone else prescribed a cranky diet for her. It is noteworthy that non-medical healers, whether spiritualistic or Charismatic, often seem to avoid facing the fact of death. This is a surprising situation, since spiritualists are especially committed to the after-life (which they tend to portray in glowing colours, except for the very evil members of society or those who are spiritually undeveloped), while Charismatics are closely involved in the resurrection of Christ and the succeeding pentecostal downflow of the Holy Spirit. In neither group should death be simply accepted as a sad termination of the present life, but rather welcomed as a time of transition of the person to a new and finer realm of endeavour! Of course, premature death cuts short the person's experience on earth, and so is to be averted as far as possible, but there comes a time for us all to make our departure, a very welcome time, I believe, at least for those of us whose lives have been devoted to our neighbour as well as to ourself. Motor neurone disease attacks the older age group, and my friend was in her early seventies – no great age nowadays, but one in which the major events of life have had time to make their impression on the character of the individual.

Despite the prognostications of the healing medium, her condition deteriorated steadily and eventually she had a frighteningly severe succession of choking attacks at home. Her visitors, aware of the medium's prohibition, were loth to consult the doctor, until someone with common sense realized how culpably ridiculous they all would look if she were to die without medical attention. And so the general practitioner was called in. He helped her through the attack, but, of course, could not influence the progress of the malady. After this event, my friend discharged the medium (who, needless to say, thrived financially from her ministrations), and enjoyed a normal diet once more. A beautiful serenity came over her; she ceased to struggle, and learned to accept each moment of life as it came. She began to know something of the peace of God that passes all understanding. She lived on for about nine months, enveloped in an aura of benediction. She stayed as active as her condition permitted; as is usual in this disease, her mind remained clear to the end. This is another distressing feature of the malady: the patient witnesses with mounting apprehension the deteriorating function of the voluntary movements of the body. But, in my friend's case, the dread had been transmuted into a peaceful co-operation with the forces of nature that were to free her at the right time of the burden of a failing body, so that the true self could enter a new plane of experience.

It would be as unfair to label all psychic healers as charlatans as to exonerate all Renewal ministers from the charge of ever having misled their flock with false claims. I have known Christian ministers of healing allegedly representing the highest ecclesiastical sources delude the dying ludicrously with assurances of complete physical recovery. Nor is the medical profession exempt from criticism; it too has its share of black sheep who batten on the sufferings of the incurably afflicted with therapies of little proven efficacy. But qualified doctors are members of a learned profession, and their actions are controlled by a general medical council that deals expeditiously with allegations of malpractice and misconduct. At the same time there are defence societies that assist their medical members, both legally and financially, when actions alleging bad or inadequate treatment have been brought against them by patients who have suffered ill-effects while under their care. Medical practitioners, in other words, are under the close scrutiny of the law, and litigation is a nightmare that keeps them fully about their business of treating their patients as efficiently and humanely as possible.

It is unfortunate that spiritual healers as well as those who use alternative therapies of various kinds do not have their own disciplinary bodies. It is also unfortunate that there is still so little dialogue between the medical profession and practitioners of alternative approaches in the vast subject of healing. One observation, however, does strike home: the conscientious doctor remembers his failures with shame, whereas the practitioner of alternative therapies (including spiritual healing) is much more likely to boast about his successes. Those who do not benefit in a tangible way soon dissolve into anonymity. The failure to improve is easily attributed to disobedience or poor faith. Is faith indeed more necessary for spiritual and alternative types of healing than for medical treatment? On one level the answer would appear clearly affirmative: drugs and surgical operations produce their predictable effects on the body (and mind) by virtue of their distinctive properties. But even here the situation is complicated by the placebo effect: even an inert preparation can produce some amelioration of symptoms if the patient believes it to be effective. Hence there is the necessity of double-blind trials to assess the efficacy of any new drug: neither the research worker who administers it nor the person who receives it knows whether the substance is in fact inert or potentially effective, so closely do the two preparations resemble one another. This form of testing allows for the psychic response between the doctor and the patient, both of whom would crave for a successful reaction for personal reasons (of compassion and also the scientific triumph over disease on the part of the doctor; of sheer relief on the part of the patient).

In fact, trust between practitioner and patient is essential in all forms of therapy, whether medical, psychological or alternative. In the last two categories of healing a deep relationship between the two is obviously important, because there must be a close psychic link between the therapist and the client for the free flow of the Holy Spirit, who is the true restorer of function. The same principle applies also to orthodox medical practice, but nowadays the powerful drug or surgical operation tends to interpose itself so categorically that the practitioner is in danger of becoming little more than a skilled diagnostician who can prescribe the appropriate treatment. The 'bedside manner' of a past generation of doctors may well be contemptuously dismissed by their successors as a mere substitute for proper treatment, but even the most effective therapy cannot by itself foster the trust built up by a close working relationship between doctor and patient. The drugs prescribed may play an invaluable role in curing the disease, but healing of the person needs something apart from this contribution: an openness of the psyche to the creative power of life which shows itself in growth, maturity and, eventually, like a ripe fruit, termination for another round of existence. These considerations may well lie outside the range of conventional medical thinking – after all, we are not all skilled metaphysicians. But then we need another class of healing ministers to repair this deficiency. It is precisely here that alternative medicine, and especially spiritual healing, may have its unique part to contribute.

The concept of holistic medicine is very topical, but its actual meaning is often blurred by prejudices and enthusiasms on the part of various practitioners. It aims at treating the person as a whole: body, mind and soul are to be integrated into a single unit by various forms of therapy. Often, unfortunately, it is the alternative contribution that dominates the intentions of the therapists, while orthodox medical practitioners stand aloof with derision from what they regard as primitive superstition, if not frank charlatanry. Since the double-blind type of trial is usually impracticable in alternative medicine, its claims to efficacy depend heavily on anecdote. This, while not to be disparaged, is too subjective to be acceptable to a scientifically detached observer. Only personal experience can truly convert him to a more sympathetic attitude. In fact, real holistic healing is more profitably understood as the open-hearted collaboration of all the various therapies in humble mutual acceptance for the good of the individual as a member of society. The one therapy does not disparage and try to supplant the other so as to demonstrate its own superiority. On the contrary, the practitioner sees his work achieving the best results when he co-operates most fully with his peers of other skills. The orthodox allopathic discipline must at present necessarily have overall charge and responsibility, because its results are far more predictable than those of other therapies, and it is remarkably effective in a steadily increasing number of bodily disorders. But it should not dominate the healing scene. Chastened by the unpleasant side-effects that from time to time mar its efforts, it should willingly take its place as first among equals rather in the fashion of the master washing the disciples' feet. It is humility alone that can bring the various agencies of healing into the union of loving service for the afflicted person and ultimately for divided humanity. Each arm of the healing ministry has its own place, but it can work effectively only in the context of the whole body.

Therefore, we should have faith in no one other than God (or the creative principle of life, for those who cannot accept a personal deity). We may have confidence in the skill of a medical practitioner and his paramedical colleagues, such as nurses, physiotherapists and psychologists, in the same way as we do in the skills of lawyers, accountants and artisans of various trades. In each instance the confidence ripens into trust if we feel a bond of emotional sympathy between them and us. This emotional sympathy deepens into psychic communion as the relationship grows in healing work. In alternative medicine this deeper fellowship is mandatory if a progressive healing is to take place. In the case of Jesus, his ability to attain such a relationship with anyone who was willing to receive him was instantaneous, and then the Holy Spirit flowing from him in unique strength could effect healings that still elude scientific explanation. And these 'miracles' occur today also, as in my own healing encounter with Constance Peters which I described earlier. Let it be said at once that this type of event cannot simply be attributed to the influence of the patient's mind on his body – an extension of so-called psychosomatic medicine. The effects are so immediate that the patient's mind is bypassed, later to be transformed as a result of the unexpected healing experience. This does not mean that 'miraculous healings' will never be open to a truly scientific explanation, but simply that the tools of science at present available are incapable of coping with these matters. Hence most scientific observers find it easiest to discredit paranormal healings, a prejudice if anything confirmed by the uncritical acclaim afforded them in both spiritualistic and Charismatic circles.

We should remember that the Holy Spirit, that Person of the Godhead who guides us progressively into all truth – such as we are able to assimilate at any one time – enlightens the understanding of the scientific research worker whether he investigates the complex structure of the body in the orthodox medical tradition or the intricacies of the mind in new fields of psychology. He fills the souls of all those who minister healing with compassion. It is only when love and compassion enter into human reckoning that the coldly intellectual thrust of so much scientific research may be deflected from sensational procedures of debatable morality to a warm regard for the sanctity of all life. God has indeed put enormous power into the human mind so that we control our domain of lesser creatures. But the power can as easily be used selfishly, and therefore destructively, as selflessly, and therefore beneficially. The field of healing from down-to-earth medical practice to the rarefied heights of spiritual ministration, illustrates this ambivalence quite starkly. But whereas medical practice can often proceed fairly satisfactorily with only slight spiritual vision, the heights of healing are intimately involved in that vision.

It may well be that humanity is now able once again to continue the healing work of Christ, so long submerged by the momentous developments in physical, chemical and biological science. Certainly a more holistic approach to health becomes increasingly necessary as orthodox medical research threatens to submerge moral considerations in a vast sea of expediency. The well-being of the sick person may in the end reside in a changed outlook rather than a restoration of a previous pattern of existence. The dispensation of spiritual healing peculiar to the apostolic period may quite probably be in the process of renewal in our obsessively materialistic society, to show us that true health lies in the transfiguration of the psyche and the resurrection of the body to spiritual excellence.

6

The Intricacies of Prayer in Healing

I frequently think of the author of the Fourth Gospel with sympathy as he leaves us with the reflection, 'There is so much else that Jesus did. If it were all to be recorded in detail, I suppose the whole world could not hold the books that would be written' (John 21:25). The subject of prayer has been considered in so many manuals devoted to the spiritual life, to say nothing of weightier theological tomes, that any fresh addition to the literature seems brash as well as otiose. Nevertheless, prayer is so intimately involved in health that any contemporary contribution can at the very least be of historical and sociological value. The Renewal Movement has centred decisively on prayer; indeed, God is told in no uncertain terms what the group requires of him. Even the caveat, 'if it is your will', has been severely criticized in some quarters, since it implies that God may not want a healing to take place, a monstrous lack of faith in those who claim that a God of love always intends the healing of his sick creatures.

In any discussion of prayer, two considerations stand out prominently: first, prayer is a personal response to the divine presence and therefore all accounts are enclosed in an individual perspective; in fact, there are as many ways of effective praying as there are people who pray. As befits the logic of mysticism, the language emphasizes 'both and/neither nor' rather than the emphatic 'either or' of Aristotelian logic. No individual, no matter how perverse his private life, is outside the divine care provided he presents himself in humble faith to receive that love. Second, since Christians affirm that God is love, a love made clear in the sacrifice of Christ for the reconciliation of the world to the Father, it is the divine intention that healing should always occur. The word 'always' may, however, embrace an indefinite time-span, since the free will of the creature can interpose itself and lead to a protracted period of delay. In his eternal mode God is all-powerful, but in the cosmic sphere he has granted freedom of choice to his rational creatures, so that they have been created minor gods in their own right – but always under the divine aegis. Were it not for this final clause, humankind would have long since destroyed itself together with the little world it inhabits. Prayer is the bond of fellowship as well as the means of communication between the human and the divine.

The agent of prayer is God, not man. His insistent presence in our lives evokes a corresponding response on our part, for he quickens our awareness both of our own inadequacies and the needs of those around us. Prayer is a built-in psychological response to the events of our lives, much as breathing is to our body's need for oxygen and the discharge of carbon dioxide from the blood. While breathing can never be voluntarily halted for more than a short period of time before the tension becomes intolerable, it is possible to banish the need for prayer from our awareness indefinitely as a result of worldly preoccupations, intellectual doubt and emotional turmoil. But in due course the desire will be so strong as to be irresistible, and we will be forced into stillness in order to listen to what we are being told in the depths of the soul. No matter what philosophical stance we may adopt, no matter how emotionally recalcitrant we may be, there is a breaking-point in our resistance to God. Quite often it is unmitigated suffering that breaks down our self-erected defences, and then at last God can enter our lives as a conscious presence. It is an extension of this principle that encourages me to hope that all evil can eventually come back, healed and transfigured, into the divine presence. But the will of the creature is inviolate.

Since, as Jesus teaches in Matthew 6:7–8, God knows our needs before we ask him, it stands to reason that we should be quiet in his presence, and listen. This action is called contemplation. It is a state of absolute awareness of the present moment, devoid of all discursive content other than the awareness itself. Do we, in fact, ever know this state of rapt awareness in the course of our active life in the world, or is it a new experience that we have to await with bated breath? It is, indeed, a common experience of everyday life, and it does not depend on any prior system of belief. We know it in any situation of sharp suspense, just before the outcome is to be revealed. It may be something rather menacing like the word of the doctor about to pronounce the possible diagnosis of a malady fraught with foreboding, such as cancer or a progressive disease of the brain. It may be more benign, as when we are awaiting the arrival of a messenger bearing news about the outcome of the choice of a selection committee – as the word comes, whether by letter or in the company of a number of applicants all sitting tensely together in a side-room, we are once again in a state of pure, undistorted awareness. Decidedly more pleasant is the suspense we know in a concert hall or at the opera just as the performance is about to start: conductor, orchestra and soloist (or cast, as the case may be) are all poised for a dramatic entry and the silence is audible in its intensity. Once we know the experience of that tense silence, we can recall and reproduce it at will, soon without any emotional colouring.

The essence of contemplation is the awareness of being aware of nothing: in this silence the One Who Is is indeed alone with us. Just as he is at our side in the menacing suspense of bad news, just as he is with us in our moment of joyful expectancy, so he is eternally present with us when we transcend the plane of images and enter the silence of self-dedication to the highest we know in the depths of our being. But we must stay aware, otherwise we will either drop off to sleep or else be assailed by emotional material stemming either from our own unconscious or from the vaster psychic realms that are in continuity with our own psyche. If such extraneous material does intrude, it should be gently but decisively swept away. If it is of importance, we can note it in a flash and give it all to the One Who Is, to whom we give the name God. In the famous words of *The Cloud of Unknowing*, 'By love may he be gotten and holden, but by thought never'. In fact, it is God's love that reaches out to us and then we are enabled to reciprocate in kind. There is no violation of persons, only a union into a greater whole in which God is master and servant at the same time, functions that we too are taught to imitate.

In this state of being our thought and emotional processes are radically cleansed, so that we can grasp something of the divine will and obey its instruction rather than simply stating our own need. In that chastening silence God shows us the nature of our real need: not so much a reversal of present discomfort as a change in our own perspective of reality, not so much the acquisition of things as the ability to use what we already have with reverence, indeed with loving awareness, so that (to enter into the thought of Martin Buber) an 'It' becomes something of a 'Thou'. In this state of awareness the demanding ego fades into the larger contours of the true self, and healing is seen more clearly as a restoration of the personality into something of the divine image in which it was originally created. The selfish preoccupation that is the basis of sinful action can be clearly defined, and as it is confessed, so its totality is brought into full consciousness. When we speak to God after having listened in the silence of contemplation, we converse with our whole being and not merely the superficial ego that effects little communication with the deeper levels of soul consciousness. Is God in any way ignorant of our inner state? Surely he cannot be, but our actions will remain a dark secret until the mystery of our individual response shows itself. Even the divine presence cannot impose itself upon the free will that is the glory of a rational creature. Experience alone teaches us that our higher good is attained when we work in harmony with God and our fellow-creatures, but much experiment in living may be necessary before that wisdom is made available to us. In prayer we can assume, take on, a wisdom that transforms our very style of living. The process is long and demanding, in fact it has no ending. But it makes our lives more and more meaningful as it increases our usefulness to God and to his creatures.

And so our petitions, fully articulated in word or thought, are our responses to God's summons to a nobler life. Our confessions follow God's revelation of our shortcomings that prevent us from doing our work properly – what we articulate we now register positively in the depths of the soul. Our intercessions serve to direct the power of the Holy Spirit to those for whom we pray. We do not need to ask so much as to love, for God knows the disposition and needs of the afflicted far better than do we. The greatest prayers in the Bible have been a simple opening of the soul to God's providence in divine ignorance yet radiant trust: Isaiah's call to ministry (Isaiah 6:8), the Annunciation (Luke 1:38), and Gethsemane (Mark 14:36). There is finally the prayer of praise: the soul's spontaneous outpouring of joy in the presence of God for the privilege of knowing that presence and being chosen to work with it in closest union. The Magnificat (Luke 1:46–55) is the most perfect expression of such praise in the Bible; it has its precursor in the song of Hannah (1 Samuel 2:1–10), which is less personal and more distant in tone. God is indeed 'the ground of our beseeching' (the foundation of our praying), as Dame Julian of Norwich puts it, but our response is equally important in the transaction. It is a measure of God's courtesy that he treats us as equals, and not simply as servants called on to do his will.

All this is important when we broach the intricacies of healing prayer. What are we really hoping to achieve in such activity? It can hardly be to enlist God's help in a difficult situation, since he is aware of it long before our attention is drawn to the problem. Jesus reminds us, in Matthew 6:7–8, that God knows our need and that lengthy prayers do not add to the power of God's providence. Indeed, much praying has a morbidly obsessional quality that merely betrays the person's lack of deeper faith. It has its counterpart in the nagging spouse or customer who doubts whether his or her requests have been noted. Nothing sours a relationship so quickly as nagging, because it implies a lack of trust that is a prerequisite of any working collaboration. If we cannot trust God to know the intimate concerns of our hearts, the trust will not be increased by anxious repetitions. In fact, it is we who fail God in our inconstancy; he is always there, but so often we are elsewhere in our thoughts. As we read in Isaiah 30:15, our safety lies in peace and our strength in stillness and in staying quiet. But just like the Israelites of old, we prefer to influence events rather than put our trust in God. This trust does not look for a miraculous solution of our problems – if this were to occur as a common event we could not grow as people, but would continue in a childish dependence on God to meet all our needs without playing our part. It is better to see prayer as a means of opening ourselves up more perfectly to the power of the Holy Spirit, who both sets in motion our own healing and works through us to our fellow-creatures, both through our intercessions and in the daily work of our calling. He strengthens us and helps us to integrate our split personalities so that we begin to function as whole people.

As we saw earlier on, our very attempts to assist God can actually interfere with his healing activity. It depends on what we do: if we are quiet and obedient, God can work well through us, but if the ego takes charge, it insidiously blocks the Holy Spirit whose action is increasingly frustrated. If we stay quiet, in trusting awareness, we can be effective ministers of healing, but as soon as the ego that looks for results gets in the way, God allows it to take charge until the baleful effects of its interference are made clear. Likewise it can be actually harmful to try to exert a telepathic influence for what we believe is good in the course of prayer. Even if the psychic influence were effective, it might simply be directing the person along paths of endeavour whose destination was not in accordance with what was required of him and therefore contrary to God's intention. What appears to be right in our own eyes may be wrong for other people. The path of acknowledged ignorance can be nearer the truth than impressive displays of psychic virtuosity or charismatic power, both of which tend to 'take over' both the agent and the object of attention.

How then should we pray for a sick person, indeed for anyone in need? By contemplating God in the silence of the present moment and remembering with solicitude the person in need. It is unnecessary to visualize the individual – quite often there is only a name given without a face to match, but this does not matter, since it is soul contact that is effected in intercessory prayer. We may be confident that the divine love plays its proper part; we assist by a loving concern that, as it were, beams the rays of God's Spirit to the place where help is required. Since our intention is that God's will be done, and we believe that God wills healing for all his creatures according to his wisdom, we do not need to refresh the memory of the Deity with details and instructions about individuals. We may indeed feel constrained to offer our articulate requests to God either mentally or in spoken words; this is unexceptionable enough so long as we understand that we alone are gaining emotional release by unburdening ourselves of our deep concern to God. In itself this dialogue does not increase the potency of the prayer, but the relief of emotional tension may help us subsequently to pray with a more concentrated, less distracted ardour. Prayer attains its peak in wordless communication with God and our neighbour. There may be great emotional exaltation, but as the zenith is attained, so all feeling is subsumed in a peace beyond understanding in which we, God, and the person prayed for are one in essence in the power of the Holy Spirit. Prayer has no finite limits; when we remember a person with loving concern in the course of a busy day's work, we are praying for him. The less aware we are of ourselves, the closer we are to the one for whom we intercede. In such self-forgetfulness God has taken his place as the director of the soul, the Father to whom all creation pours out paeans of unceasing praise.

Whenever we perform an action in mindful awareness of the divine presence we are in fact in a state of prayer. This is the ideal prayer life, to be constantly about God's business in joyful abandon. This is the full constancy of prayer that St Paul enjoins on his followers (1 Thessalonians 5:17). It is the song of a soul set free from the thraldom of material things, flying high in the heavens and yet still in control of worldly affairs.

In some intercessory groups the various members take it in turns to pray for a sick person, so that he is 'soaked' with prayer throughout the day. All this is admirable provided we do not use prayer as a way of trying to bludgeon God into doing what we desire. Such a prayer can be well-nigh obsessional in its intensity, allowing God little time for repose from the work with which the group is concerned! Prayer in itself is in danger of becoming warped once it loses its joyful spontaneity and becomes a mere instrument of calculated human desire, no matter how laudable that desire may be, at least on the surface. What often passes for prayer is in fact psychic coercion; it is possible for a person of indifferent spirituality but with a highly charged emotional nature to tap into a psychic reservoir and draw out the material substance he desires. Such a way of appeasing inner needs is too closely related to psychically evil forces for our comfort. The person himself tends to arrogance and self-assurance, but soon less pleasant episodes warn him of the dangerous company he is keeping. As we have already noted, the Antichrist figure starts by satisfying the needs of the masses so that they soon enlist themselves as ready vassals to their glittering master.

Prayer, too, if misconceived, can communicate with very questionable sources in the intangible, astral realms. No wonder Jesus told Martha that the pure contemplation practised by her sister Mary was the better way of life. It does not strain after results or yield to temptations of impatience or boastfulness. It alone is the foundation of the communion of God and man which we call prayer. And so it comes about that prayer is simple enough to lie within the reach of the little child (which we all have to become if we are to enter the Kingdom of heaven) and yet so intricate as to be outside the range of many intellectually scintillating people. Indeed, until their brilliance and conceit have been laid aside, often only after misfortune has stripped them of all earthly assurance, they will remain blind to the greater reality that is God.

Most of the so-called techniques of prayer are in fact ways of stilling the stream of thoughts and their accompanying emotional charge: the repetition of a phrase or a single word (a mantra), the non-rational language of ecstatic utterance ('tongues'), the calm meditation on a passage of Scripture or a piece of music, or the simple awareness of a body rhythm (breathing). The articulated prayers of the various religious traditions of the world, of which the Lord's Prayer is the most universal Christian example, also help to still the mind of extraneous thoughts if they are said slowly and with meaning. More often they are recited mechanically, and the worshipper then feels he has said his prayers for the day quite adequately! If the act of worship brings us to God in humble adoration, the practice of prayer opens us to dialogue with him. The end of the meeting is our own progressive healing so that we can be about our Father's business selflessly and with profit to the world. He who knows the divine presence as a living relationship within himself and in the world around himself has attained the ultimate knowledge. Whatever work he may then undertake will be blessed in its very performance, and its results will likewise be blessed even if much pain and suffering are to be encountered on the way. 'In the world you will have trouble. But courage! The victory is mine; I have conquered the world' (John 16:33). This is the heart of the matter. Healing will be complete only when one has entered into the fullness of one's inheritance as a brother of Christ himself. All other healings are, at most, signs on the way to completeness, but they can just as easily, by becoming ends in their own right, prevent us from attaining the ultimate victory over the darkness within ourselves. And so the type of mentality that tries to prove God by positive answers to prayer or the results of a healing service in church, has hardly a nodding acquaintance with the Lord of all life. 'You are not to put the Lord your God to the test' (Deuteronomy 6:16 and repeated by Christ in Matthew 4:7 and Luke 4:12), is the key text here, but how seldom do we heed it! When we work in calm trust, each minute has its own blessing to share. When we work in urgent anticipation, we are very likely to be sadly disappointed. The reason is, as already stated, that the selfish ego interposes itself between God and the greater good which he alone knows, and the power of the Holy Spirit is deflected from its proper end to be dissipated in fruitless emotional distractions.

Meditation is nowadays widely canvassed even among those who have no spiritual aspirations. On a purely medical level this is to be welcomed. Relaxation of the body counters the effects of stress so widespread in a competitive, materialistic society. Meditation enables the mind to relax also, at least to the extent of letting go of destructive thoughts and transcending disturbing emotional states. It can be the precursor of contemplation, and indeed in Hindu and Buddhist circles the concept of meditation is identical with the contemplation practised in Christian groups and whose nature we have already discussed. It is not necessarily the same as prayer, however, because it lacks the commitment to God and his service that is the basis of praying. Nevertheless, an agnostic meditator in the Hindu-Buddhist mode may well encounter God in the depths of his stillness, and then contemplative prayer may be initiated. We remember that the personal God of the three Semitic religions is not acknowledged and worshipped in the Buddhist way (or in some of the various Hindu systems either). But the experience is probably one – the difference lies in its interpretation, and here we are wise to respect other insights and in humility learn from them all. This is not an invitation to syncretism (the production of a hybrid faith with accretions from various sources) but, rather, a broadening of one's own particular beliefs through encounter with other traditions. In the end one's own fundamental point of view remains intact but considerably more enlightened than previously: one understands better what one really does believe, seeing both the strengths and the weaknesses of other traditions in the process of learning – and also the problems of one's own tradition.

Cancer patients are frequently taught the basis of meditation when they visit centres that provide alternative means of treatment, especially when the disease is so advanced as to be difficult to eradicate by the conventional medical therapies at present available. A recommended theme of meditation (in the Western rather than the Eastern understanding of the word) is the visualization of the body's defence cells, the phagocytes, attacking and destroying the cancer cells. There are some who claim that this type of meditation does actually assist the body to overcome the disease; but it must be acknowledged that the meditation can be quite taxing, especially to a debilitated person, and if the results are unimpressive, there may be disappointment tinged with guilt that the procedure was not adequately pursued to its required intensity. And so any possible benefit can easily be annulled by fatigue and reversed by disillusion if no obvious results are forthcoming. In desperate situations any type of therapy that offers even a thread of hope is grasped with alacrity, but the claims of the various alternative modes of treatment, especially in as variable a condition as cancer, still await scientific confirmation. While most types of cancer proceed inexorably to a fatal conclusion if they are not completely eradicated, a few may remain stationary for considerable periods of time. Furthermore, there is also the rare but spectacular 'spontaneous remission', in which the tumour suddenly, and for no apparent reason, disappears completely, sometimes never to appear again. It may be that some such remissions are consequent on spiritual healing wrought by prayer, but it would be impossible, in terms of our present knowledge, to provide a categorical explanation of this fascinating phenomenon.

An alternative type of meditation in situations of medically incurable disease is the simple contemplation already described. One can either be quite still before God, offering him one's soul and body for the healing that he knows is appropriate for one's condition, or else imagine the Holy Spirit being drawn into one's body with each inspiration. The air is an established symbol of the Holy Spirit, as Jesus tells Nicodemus in their wonderful nocturnal discourse (John 3:8): like the wind, the Spirit blows where it wills; we can hear it, but we do not know where it comes from or whither it is going. Acceptance can be the best form of defence, especially when we are confronted by well-nigh insuperable forces of destruction. The head-on attack of allopathic medicine may finally register a gallant defeat, after which the very forces of death could be converted to the light by a greater power of

God that infused the soul and renewed the body with new life. This might conceivably be the spiritual background to the authenticated cases of spontaneous remission of cancer. Even if this were the case, one would expect to find demonstrable changes in the body's immune system occurring side by side with the disappearance of the tumour deposits. In healing there is always a close correlation of the various aspects of the personality – of body and soul – so that a change in one is reflected on a wider front irrespective of where the process began. Healing is indeed a fully incarnational phenomenon.

There are some healers, quite often of Hindu background, that project their presence psychically either directly onto the person they have been called on to heal or else in the surroundings of his home. The process may be related to what is called 'astral travelling' (the movement of the essence, or soul, of a person to distant realms in a sphere outside normal time and space). All this may be immediately reassuring, as the healer may himself live far away, perhaps in India, while his client has a European domicile. The psychic virtuoso (for that is what he is, and there need be no conspicuous spiritual component to his personality) may show himself directly as a 'phantasm of the living', to quote the title of a famous classic of psychical research by Edmund Gurney, F. W. H. Myers and Frank Podmore, published in 1886. Sometimes there may instead be a simpler sensory manifestation, such as a strong scent of flowers, that heralds his presence. However, once the presence is registered, it often shows no intention of departing. It is as if the healer were claiming the total allegiance of the person who called for help. Escape can be fraught with great difficulties so that the ministry of deliverance (exorcism) may sometimes be necessary to sever the psychic link and send the healer back to where he lives on an earthly plane. All this again stresses the close involvement of strong psychic forces in much of the ministry of healing; these forces are not in themselves evil, but they require constant supervision lest they intrude upon areas where they should not have free access.

The wise practitioner bypasses their distracting clamour

by contemplative prayer to God, who then enables him to harness pervasive, morally neutral psychic powers under the direction of the Holy Spirit in order to effect healing changes (and also the other gifts of the Spirit mentioned in 1 Corinthians 12:1–11). In other words, our allegiance should be to God alone and not to any intermediate power that may play its part in the total process of healing. This applies equally to human personalities and the 'masters' revered by esotericists. There is never any need to belittle the belief systems of other groups of seekers – all of whom are probably grasping some small organ of truth – provided our own sight is fixed on the One from whom all good things proceed, remembering that for those who love him, all things work together for good.

7

The Price of Healing

Healing is a gift of God. Just as the repair process of the body proceeds with unhurried speed on its own – assisted by medical and alternative means as the occasion arises – so the flow of healing power that infuses the minister comes as pure grace, an unmerited gift, to and through him to his neighbour in need. God's nature is unceasing self-giving, seen in Christian terms in the sacrifice of Jesus for the restoration of the fallen world, for its reconciliation to God, who lowers himself to take on an earthly form so as to enter into the full extent of pain and suffering that is the lot of the mortal creature.

To whom the gift of healing flows, the power of Christ descends. The minister is God's servant, and at once he assumes the Master's mantle as did Elisha that of Elijah. The mantle establishes his authority, but it also encloses a share of prophetic reponsibility: to whom much is given, much is expected. A gift not generously distributed to the world rapidly turns sour in the one who is its steward, corrupting his personality with vain imaginings of supremacy with its attendant grandeur. This is the price of the gift: the burden of its use in an indifferent world that treads its pearls into the mud of garish sensationalism and thoughtless ingratitude. The people do not know what they are doing to the minister, but his gift must continue to be circulated.

There is a price to be paid by both the minister and the one he treats. The price demanded of the minister is an immaculate life-style: decency in his behaviour and chastity in his private living. It could be objected at once that many successful healers lead lives of gross indiscipline – among their members there are those who eat, drink and smoke too much and also some whose sexual habits are far from exemplary. But their peculiar gift is a surface, contact one, and indeed many of their number typify the ministry Jesus himself might have enjoyed had he submitted to the satanic temptations of performing miracles in the wilderness. His psychic powers could indeed have turned stones into bread and demonstrated remarkable ascendancy over the natural order so as to assert his mastery in the world. In the end he would have been shown as a psychic virtuoso of the type we have already considered; his master would have been the devil, the prince of lies capable of seducing the very elect when they discard prayer and cultivate self-assertive mental powers. This rather round condemnation does not imply that contact healing is itself a bad thing, but simply that it is morally neutral. Like the various physical and intellectual gifts that illuminate individual personality, it can be used selfishly or wisely: for the practitioner's own ends or for the good of the greater community. If it is indeed spiritually based, dedicated to God and to one's fellow-creatures without price or reservation, it is its own blessing both to the giver and to those who receive.

In no field is the wariness of the serpent and the innocence of the dove (to quote Matthew 10:16) as necessary as in healing work, because irrespective of the minister's spiritual allegiance, there is a strong involvement of psychic forces in the operations. It seems that the Holy Spirit works through the vast angelic hosts as well as the Communion of Saints; according to the person's character, he is likely to draw to himself the corresponding intermediary agents: a selfish disposition brings him close to the forces of evil, whereas a selfless one will draw to him the powers of light that illuminate his path and direct him in the way of resurrection. We do not need to command the forces in the intermediate psychic zone; all that is required of us is a purity of intent that allows

75

the forces of light to enter and transfigure us as a preliminary to our healing work with others on the way.

The minister of healing gives allegiance to God alone, not to any earthly power nor to any intermediary entity in the psychic dimension. Both the spiritualist and the esotericist tend to be too closely involved in this area with their guides and masters to whose existence we have already alluded, so that they block the presence of the Deity. It may well be that both guide and master have an objective reality, but if they are sincerely on the side of light, they will point away from themselves to the One who is the source of all that exists. The minister of Renewal is, however, equally flawed even if he has no doubt that the power infusing him is the very Spirit of God. As we read in 1 John 4:1–3, we should not trust any and every spirit, but should rather test them to see whether they are of God or the evil one, for among those who have gone out into the world there are many falsely inspired prophets.

The true spirit acknowledges the incarnation of Christ, whereas the false one makes no such profession of faith. The true spirit, in fact, does not simply make a theological affirmation; his gentle, loving nature leads the person in the way of Christ, so that he becomes a true exemplar of the Lord in his life of love, joy and peace that flows out to the whole created universe. As St Teresa of Avila admonished herself and her community, 'Remember, Christ has no body now on earth but yours, no hands but yours, no feet but yours; yours are the eyes through which is to look out Christ's compassion to the world; yours are the feet with which he is to go about doing good, and yours are the hands with which he is to bless us now'. This is the authentic spirit of healing. If the minister brings the light of God into the lives of those whom he tends, he is indeed inspired by the Holy Spirit. Such a person is himself holy: in him God works and shows himself, so that through the minister the congregation is made holy also.

This picture of the holy one can seem almost outside the range of ordinary humanity in its spiritual demands and aspiration, but its form should gradually embrace and transfigure the personalities of all who are doing God's work in a materialistic universe. If a person with a healing gift works on his own without reference to a guiding community of some soundly based religious denomination, he may for a time flourish, but in due course he tends to become very isolated, not only in his style of living but also from the trends of contemporary society as well as universal spirituality. This tendency was very obvious in one of my mentors, Ronald Beesley, whom I mentioned earlier on. Unlike many individualistic healers, he maintained a strictly chaste way of life – indeed, as is so common in this type of situation, he had continually to evade the fulsome embraces of admirers, mostly women, that would have effectively strangled his work. He was supported unceasingly by a small team of devoted helpers, for his exquisite psychic sensitivity drove him away from the masses. Nevertheless, his teaching, excellent as it was (coming from purely inspirational sources), could have been broadened with profit had he been more involved in the spiritual scene around him. To be sure, he knew enough about the obduracy of the Church from his experiences as a youth, and in addition there was no conspicuously spiritual congregation near him, but he could nevertheless have been strengthened and enlightened by more participation in worship with a rank-and-file body of believers. I have no doubt that Jesus himself learned much from the folk around him, including the sinners at the festivities he attended, in his daily ministry. A good teacher not only gives forth the doctrine but is also prepared to receive the impact it makes on his audience – and a bad impact is often more enlightening than fulsome flattery by unthinking devotees who hang precariously on each word proceeding from the mouth of the master.

The price exacted from the healing minister is ceaseless humility, and there are few in the field who can truly understand this. The medical practitioner, as a rule, is naïvely assured of his mastery, and he seldom manages to communicate with his patient on any level other than sharp authority, tinged on occasion with kindly condescension. Personal experience of illness, often in his own family, together with increasing age tends to soften this imperious attitude. Those involved in alternative therapies start by being less dogmatic – quite often they are led into this area of practice through personal misfortune that has opened their eyes to the inadequacy of the orthodox medical approach. Whatever may be the effectiveness of their particular therapy, they too may become intolerant of criticism, since their particular approach can easily become an idol. But it is in the realm of 'spiritual healing' that dogmatism frequently attains its peak, as it did to a considerable extent in the instance of Ronald Beesley. The metaphysical stance of the practitioner becomes his means of identification and sometimes his very god. This is especially the case of those healing ministers who have a strongly religious base. God becomes their servant, and they often judge others according to the narrow tenets of their faith. It is only when their credal god apparently fails them – as when a client dies despite all their ministrations and prayers – that the true God reveals himself to them as he did to the Prodigal Son in his moment of destitution. Only when they know that all they believed is vain, can that belief blossom into an understanding that illuminates the portals of their mind so that they can at last see the Living God. The Job experience is a necessary part of the growth of all authentic healing ministers. This theme can be stated in another way: the ego of the healing minister must be absolutely thrown into silence before the light of God can truly illuminate his personality and transfigure his gift to universal service.

It comes about that the individualistic type of healer has to be reconciled more and more with the sources of religious orthodoxy around him in order to broaden his sympathies, while the religiously connected minister of healing has to shed much of his unthinking conventionality and enter the wilderness of contemplative solitude. Truth is not to be found exclusively either in the halls of religion or the teachings of a particular group of practitioners. God alone is truth, as he is also love and beauty. Religious observances and esoteric doctrines may both show the way to the ultimate being of God, as may also orthodox medical practice in a more earthly way; indeed, they form a trinity of approach to the divine presence, and any one is not to be exalted above the other two. But God is above all forms and ideologies. He nearly always shows himself when the mind is completely open to the present moment, knowing only that it knows nothing. All human practices have to be eclipsed by the cloud of dark divinity (similar to the cloud that filled the temple of Jerusalem when Isaiah received his call to ministry, or the cloud into which Christ was taken up at the moment of his ascension to the Father) before their intentions are healed of sectarian animosity. It is at this point that full healing occurs, primarily of the individual but ultimately of the wider community also.

Therefore it comes about that the healing ministry demands an aspiring integrity on the part of those practising it, so that their innocence may be the way of the knowledge of God for all who encounter them. There is no price, no charge, for who could demand payment for a divine gift! It could be in order for an uncommitted contact healer and also one involved in esoteric pursuits to claim recompense, for they are using an essentially natural gift for the benefit of those who require their help. But a truly spiritual healer has had his gift consecrated in the presence of God so that it attains a stamp of divine authority. The natural psychic talent has become fully spiritualized, even divinized, and so its true master is God alone. 'Have no fear, little flock; for your Father has chosen to give you the Kingdom' (Luke 12:32). The passage continues with the admonition to sell our possessions and give to charity, providing ourselves with purses that do not wear out and never-failing treasure in heaven, beyond the reach of intruding thief or destructive moth. Where our treasure is, there also will be our heart. The virtuous Rich Young Man could not make this gesture of faith, whereas the venal tax-gatherer Zacchaeus could do it without request once he had received healing forgiveness from Christ.

In any situation of spiritual fellowship the experience of mutual sharing on the deepest level is its own reward. It is for this reason that the spiritual aspirant looks neither for personal reward nor for positive results of his actions. He has been afforded the privilege of conveying the Holy Spirit to those around him, and in turn the same Spirit flows with redoubled strength to him and through him. Of course, it may be insisted that we all, no matter how spiritual may be our aspirations, have to keep body and soul together. Jesus tells us to set our minds on God's Kingdom and his justice before everything else, and all the rest that we need for everyday existence such as food, drink and clothing, will come to us as well. In practical terms this promises that we will be able to ply our particular trade or occupation with so improved a standard of performance and with such excellent results that our material problems will be solved by our own efforts, fully infused as we are by the Holy Spirit who is God's special gift to us. In other words, our daily work will provide our financial support: some of us may be professional ministers of religion and others industrious laymen with our own particular sources of income. I have no doubt that it is inadvisable to depend on a healing gift for one's subsistence, unless the practice is embraced in a professional counselling or psychotherapeutic ambience. A healing practice is bound to demand results if money is exchanged, and the strain on the conscientious minister can be intolerable. Less scrupulous healers have little compunction in battening on incurably ill people, like the medium who rejected doctors in the case of motor neurone disease afflicting a friend that I have already described. I have known similar situations in frightened people with retinitis pigmentosa, an hereditary eye disease that leads inexorably to progressive visual loss in youth. Money has been paid, but as might have been expected, there was no improvement in sight. When I am involved in such a situation, I do all I can to heal in the name of God, but the real healing comes from the relationship struck with the disquieted person, so that whatever may transpire in the future, he at least knows he has a friend at hand who will not let him down. Needless to say, there is no charge for this service. To be fair to many healers, it is ignorance as much as greed that directs their efforts to the incurably ill whom they are not helping. Hope springs eternal in the hearts of healer and client alike. But at least one should know what one is doing under such circumstances.

The vagaries of the healing ministry are immense. Jesus healed many people, but he was not able to heal himself when he hung crucified between two criminals. St Paul, the great proponent of the doctrine of justification by faith, must have been God's instrument for the healing of many people around him. And yet his own 'thorn in the flesh' (identified by some as a sharp physical pain or some other equally incapacitating malady) stayed with him. He prayed for release on three occasions, but to no avail. Nevertheless, the message he received was worth more than any physical relief: 'My grace is all you need; power comes to its full strength in weakness' (2 Corinthians 12:7–9). He goes on to affirm his joy in the things that are his weakness, for when he is weak, then is he strong. Personally I am relieved that the great Apostle to the Gentiles did not receive a healing, for now he is a witness to the many sick people who also have to proceed as best they can, unrelieved by any of the available healing agencies. The humiliation of his malady cut Paul down to size when he had had a not infrequent mystical insight into the nature of reality, or when he had scathingly rebuked his obtuse disciples a little too ferociously. Then he remembered that he too had been a persecutor of the Christian community at an earlier period.

In healing work it is not uncommon for some distinctly peripheral person to get relief while the pillars of the community remain untouched. Why did I, a mere visitor to Constance Peters' group, receive a dramatic healing while her longstanding supporters did not have any spectacular manifestation? Perhaps it was because my own participation in the ministry of healing was imminent, and I required both the experience of a personal healing and a demonstration of the way I was to proceed in the future. Certainly people who have been the recipients of remarkable healings, whether at church services or in the personal ministry of a practitioner, not infrequently are converted to God in Christ, and have played their part subsequently in furthering the ministry. But sometimes 'Christ' is a universal power behind all creation (the cosmic Christ) rather than the personal presence beloved by the committed Christian. In life both aspects of the Logos have to be integrated: incarnation is to be universalized, for no one knows the full measure of God. Whatever we say speaks more about ourselves than about the Deity, who shows himself in the world of created forms as Father, Son and Holy Spirit, but whose essence is concealed in the cloud of unknowing. On the other hand, the Godhead can remain an intriguing philosophical category until it is incarnated in the lives of ordinary people; God was in Christ reconciling the world to himself (2 Corinthians 5:19). It is certain that the true minister of healing has to 'put on Christ', as St Paul would say (Galatians 3:27).

The recipient of healing also has a price to pay: a new life dedicated to the Highest. Even if he cannot accept the concept of a personal God, his life should be guided by the highest values which are summed up in personal integrity. The last five of the Ten Commandments are a useful series of guidelines: inflicting no hurt on our fellow-creatures by killing (including character assassination and cruelly destructive criticism), committing adultery, stealing (including the appropriation of other people's ideas without due acknowledgement), lying with hurtful intent, and grasping after other people's possessions. As St Paul reminds us, it is only by love that these requirements of the good life can be met, since a person of love could not possibly hurt anyone else for selfish reasons. Love, too, has its severe side, for it must unmask all that is inadequate for the sake of the beloved. 'My son, do not spurn the Lord's correction or take offence at his reproof; for those whom he loves the Lord reproves, and he punishes a favourite son' (Proverbs 3:11–12). In other words, love is not soft and sentimental, let alone biased and untruthful.

It is probable that much misfortune is the result of personal inadequacy in the past – a less severe term than sin, which all too often has overtones of pious judgement by those who are no better inwardly than the victim of the affliction. But the experience of the pain and the joy of its relief can be the way forward to the new life of personal integrity which is the measure of a true healing experience. Other examples of misfortune cannot in honesty be ascribed to personal failings on the part of the afflicted ones, but are simply part of the collective, communal life we are bound to know and the responsibility that accrues from that participation. Here the innocent person (if indeed there are any completely innocent ones in the life of eternity) discovers the privilege of bearing the pain of the collective multitude for the sake of its spiritual evolution. All this gradually dawns on the sufferer as he transcends the phase of rebellion and enters into a greater relationship with all that lies around him. At last the scales can drop off his eyes, and he may see fully for the first time in his life. The lesson may be hard but the prize is beyond price, as Job learned at the end of his strange saga. The minister of healing plays his greatest role in being with the afflicted one in his travail. The healing art is, paradoxically, often at its noblest when no manifest change is wrought on a bodily level and the minister enters into creative suffering with the one he tends. This is the supreme privilege of the ministry – and also of the affliction, though, of course, the sufferer would be unable to see it in this light at the dark time of his agony. The gift is recognized later, usually in the life that stretches before us all after death.

The way of personal integrity starts with awareness born of gratitude for the gift that has been received. In a famous healing episode recorded in the Gospel, Jesus cured ten men of a repulsive skin disease, but only one, an outcast Samaritan, had the awareness to thank God for what he had received; the other nine went on their way completely absorbed in themselves, almost as if nothing unusual had happened. In the Parable of the Good Samaritan, the priest and the Levite pass on the other side of the road where a man lies beaten up by robbers. His presence impinged marginally on their awareness, and in any case they were too busy with their own thoughts to pay much attention to his plight. It was once again an outcast Samaritan who took pity on the man, because he saw him with awareness and could easily identify himself with him.

Cleansed awareness is the way forward to a dedication of one's life to God and one's fellow-creatures. In the end the one who has been healed should become a minister of healing in his own right. This does not mean so much entering into a healing practice as being a focus of healing for all those around one. I know too many self-styled healers who deplete everyone in their vicinity by their very presence. It is ironical that some of these depleters have considerable theoretical spiritual knowledge, often priding themselves on it and tending to judge others from a self-appointed seat of authority. Anyone who is ill, however, learns to dread their entry into the sickroom. By contrast, the true agent of healing gives profligately of himself by his very presence; Jesus being drained by the touch of the woman with a bleeding condition of the womb is a classical example of such constantly available healing power. As the recipient enters a new dimension of health, so he ought to be able to give something of what he has received in the course of his daily work when his thoughts are directed to the matters immediately confronting him. He is centred less on his ego and more on his soul, which is in psychic contact with the souls of all other people. We are indeed in a state of psychic osmosis with the created whole, so that anything that affects even a single person cannot fail to have repercussions on the wider body of humanity and indeed of all creation.

The life-style of the one who has received a healing grace should be simpler than before. Simplicity is a lovely virtue. It is unencumbered and entire of itself, needing no accretion to complete it, pure and undefiled. His diet should be wholesome but plain, appetizing but not stimulating the senses or dulling the mind. Many spiritual aspirants favour a vegetarian type of diet, as much as a protest against animal slaughter as for a cleansing and heightening of psychical acuity and function. Others, no less dedicated, do not reject meat, though, on the whole, they find it best to restrict their intake to white meat and fish in addition to dairy produce, vegetables and fruit. In some cancer support groups a taxing diet is (or has been) prescribed – taxing both to prepare and to eat. It needs to be said, however, that currently there is no scientific evidence of any special diet benefiting the various diseases at present beyond the help of orthodox medical treatment. Apart from the simplicity already commended, it is best for an ailing person to eat what he prefers, but always in moderation. The Edwardian music-hall artiste Marie Lloyd had it right in the title of one of her songs: a little of what you fancy does you good. A friend of mine, of profound spirituality, suffered such severe stomach injuries during the Second World War that she is unable to digest vegetarian fare, but has survived precariously on a diet consisting largely of red meat, especially steak. As long as we can control the various commodities entering our field of consciousness, whether food and drink, conversation, entertainment or art, we shall not go far astray; hedonistic gluttony on the one hand, and bizarre, cranky diets on the other take their toll of a person's health. The body has its own inbuilt wisdom which far too often is violated in adult life by the habits of smoking, alcohol abuse, gluttony, and also a neglect of eating in the face of the various tensions of living that we all experience in one form or another.

If one lives simply, one has a greater reserve of strength for the really important issues of life and death. Less time and energy are expended in emotional turmoil as well as bodily ill-health. Attached to God, as Jesus says, we need not strive for other things to fulfil us, whether they be possessions, reputation or even human relationships. They pour down upon us as a blessing the less we covet them. I take great comfort from the oracle of Malachi 3:10: 'Put me to the proof, says the Lord of Hosts, and see if I do not open windows in the sky and pour a blessing on you as long as there is need.' The relationship is the blessing, and its fruits are abundant in the new life of sober awareness and grateful dedication to God and to one's neighbour.

8

There is a Time

'For everything its season, and for every activity under heaven its time: a time to be born and a time to die,' begins the third chapter of the Book of Ecclesiastes. In the exultation of life's busy clamour we soon overlook the fact of our mortality, the brief apportioned span of experience here before we make our individual departure and move onwards. Onward movement is the essence of life, while the process of growth involves our learning from each experience, our assimilation of each encounter as it impinges upon us. The end of our mortal life is the development of a rounded personality, fulfilled in its own uniqueness and ceaselessly available for service to all who call upon it in pain and suffering. The healing ministry attains its peak of endeavour when it enables the person to enter into the divine nature of his creation, so that he may reveal something of that glorious heritage which is then contributed to the world around him. The end of fulfilled human life is a progressive spiritualization of society, seen in its most exalted form as the entire creation.

There are three resurrection miracles of Christ recorded in the Gospel: the widow of Nain's son, Jairus' daughter, and, most spectacular of them all, the long-deceased Lazarus. Why did Jesus perform these miracles? Presumably because the victim in question had not lived out his or her allotted span, and there was more to learn and to achieve before a definitively final transition. Whether the first two were instances of 'clinical death' as opposed to the later irreversible decease of the body, we do not know, and in any case the matter is somewhat theoretical. Lazarus had been entombed for four days, and his resurrection was clearly a miracle. However, the really important circumstance in all of these instances was the new understanding of reality that must have dawned on these people at the time of their resurrection. The near-death experience occurring in 'clinically dead' people (usually victims of severe heart attacks) opens their inner sight to a modality of existence distinctly beyond the range of customary human perception. They see something of the divine, however they may describe it, and with that vision there comes a grasp of the immediate importance of using their time on earth profitably, so that when they are ready to depart, perhaps many years later, they will have done what they had been sent to achieve at the time of their conception: to bring their talents back to God, hard-worn but resplendent through their dedicated usage among the people with whom their stewards once lived.

Much of my own healing work, the most significant proportion in my opinion, has been concerned with the incurably ill who are in the process of dying. In the great majority of cases the cause of the trouble has been cancer, since this disease, apart from the unusual exceptions that I have already mentioned, tends relentlessly to the destruction of the body's substance and its death if it cannot be completely eradicated at an early stage of its development. Quite often people seek my help only when the condition is far advanced in its spread, and then a remarkably fulfilling ministry frequently follows. One notable instance was that of Teresa, a woman of late middle age. Of very reserved disposition, she was before my time quite an active member of the congregation of my church. Latterly she had moved some distance away from the parish, but still maintained a loose association in memory of a previous incumbent whom she much esteemed. Only occasionally did she now attend services, and I assumed she was going to a more conveniently situated church in her immediate locality – as was indeed the case. She was not the kind of person one would approach with temerity, because of her great reticence. However, early one Sunday morning a note awaited me: Teresa was in hospital with terminal breast cancer, and she wanted me to give a message to a member of the congregation with regard to some work she could not herself perform. As soon as the morning church service had ended, I visited her in the specialized cancer hospital situated in an outlying London suburb. She was both delighted and moved to see me (moved because I had obviously forgone my lunch in order to be with her as soon as possible). She had considerable difficulty in breathing and needed intermittent oxygen, but we could communicate quite well, and I ended my visit with the laying-on of hands and prayer.

Teresa's condition slowly but steadily became stabilized, and then there was a great improvement, while we two were entering into a deep friendship, a situation unimaginable before the tragedy struck. I asked her why she had not told me about the illness much earlier on, but in fact it was her reticence that had blocked any communication – and of course she now worshipped locally. She confided that her heart really lay in my church and not in her local one, and she made it clear that she wanted the funeral service to be conducted there, giving me details about hymns and readings. She rallied sufficiently to go back to the hospice from which she had been sent to the cancer hospital, only then to develop an acute obstruction of the intestine. This is a most painful condition that soon leads to death unless it is treated surgically at once. Despite the underlying disease, the doctors and Teresa opted for an exploratory operation, which showed an obstruction at the lower part of the colon, possibly due to deposits of the tumour there. At any rate, a colostomy was performed; it relieved the obstruction completely, and soon Teresa had learned how to control it, an impressive feat in a terminally ill patient. It was evident that the cancer had gone into temporary remission, while Teresa and I were growing ever closer in friendship. In due course she left the cancer hospital for a second time to return to the hospice. There the tumour became active once more and she died about three weeks later.

There can be no doubt that this final encounter was an

important chapter in the saga of Teresa's growth of personality up to the next stage, which she is now experiencing. She
was able to open herself to me in a way that would have been
inconceivable prior to her illness, a fact brought into the open
in the diary she kept so assiduously (of course I did not read
her private jottings, but was told later by her sister how very
much Teresa had valued my constant caring). Her body was
in fact interred in the family grave in the country, but I had
the privilege of officiating at the service of thanksgiving in
my church, where the hymns and readings she had chosen
were used. I felt that I had been parted from an old friend
as I commended her soul to the light of God's love.

Was it right that an exploratory abdominal operation
should have been performed on a terminally ill woman? There
can be no definitive answer to this question, but in this
particular instance I have no doubt that the correct path had
been trod. It was good that Teresa had had this short period
of remission to enjoy (as far as any person with advanced
malignant disease can be said to enjoy the experience) and
also the colostomy to control. She had learnt to love herself
in a way that would have been impossible before the final
experience. I have been told by other colostomy subjects that
only when they give their strange guest a name can they
really tolerate and eventually love it as themselves. This artificial anus opening on to the front of the abdominal wall and
discharging faeces can be a most repulsive burden to the
squeamish, while a loving friend to those whose lives have
been prolonged by it.

A person especially beloved to me was another parishioner,
Elizabeth, who, unlike Teresa, remained a pillar of my
church. Like a number of other members of my congregation,
her religious creed was broad to a degree that would have
brought an intolerant pastor close to despair, for she had a
warm heart. It is those like her who are the real salt of the
Faith, for they can somehow live within its dogmatic structure
without excluding the greater Lord, whose nature is mercy
and whose outpouring is love for all people of all faiths. She
loved the parish church which she and her husband, an

amateur artist of great distinction, served with much devotion.

I was appointed assistant priest some time after the death of her husband, and a warm relationship sprang up between us – at that time she was in her mid-seventies and I in my early fifties. She had the sensitivity peculiar to very noble people not to intrude into my private affairs, even when she would dearly have loved to plumb the depths of my inner life. Some years later I was put in charge of the church, and depended even more on the help of Elizabeth and a few other dedicated parishioners. A little while later I became seriously ill after an accident that involved severe injuries to both shoulders. I was both physically incapacitated and mentally depressed, certainly in no condition to look after myself as I had done for nearly all my adult life. Elizabeth at once offered me hospitality in her delightful house (lent her by a rich relation, for she herself was of modest means) where I was able to make a slow recovery, interrupted by a further spell in hospital. It was very fortunate that she lived within easy walking distance of the church, for my private flat (I did not have the usual church accommodation) was a mile and a half away. How good it was, in addition, to be with her, to share her tastes and enjoy her tolerance and kindly sense of humour! She was not an intellectual, but her spiritual outlook was truly catholic and none the worse for its hospitality towards unusual ideas (how often can traditionally orthodox teachings become distasteful in the hands of the complacently intolerant believer, so that in the end they emit not so much the odour of sanctity as the stench of decay!). Her sympathies, rather like mine, were universal in scope, seeing the good rather than the evil in other people, systems of thought and religious traditions, and yet at heart being firmly rooted in Christ whom we know as a universal presence as well as an incarnated being. 'The glory of God is a man fully alive', wrote St Irenaeus. Both Elizabeth and I knew intuitively that that truly living man was Jesus of Nazareth, who has to become fully incarnated in each one of us rather than simply idolized from afar. Elizabeth also loved animals and gardens, indeed all living creatures. It was a wonderful experience to share spiritual intimacy with a person who would never have imagined herself as anything so precious as an agent of the light.

In late January 1985, we attended an afternoon cinema performance, and as we were leaving at the end, Elizabeth slipped on some stairs and strained her back. She was obliged forthwith to enter hospital for investigation and treatment, while I was smartly ejected from the comfort of her home to fend for myself in my own flat once more. Had circumstances not thus forced me to leave her home, it would have been deceptively easy and pleasant, for both of us, that I should remain indefinitely, simply using my flat as a centre for the ministry of counselling and healing. Providence acts in strange ways, uncomfortably often, but with decisive authority; and so I resumed my private existence quietly, soon putting my past troubles behind me and proceeding onwards with the usual work at home, in church, and at various conferences and retreat centres.

But Elizabeth's future was less rosy. As I got better, so she declined. It became evident that, in addition to the comparatively simple back strain, she had a disease of the right kidney, which was removed surgically some little while later. There was a stone in the ureter (the duct by which urine passes from the kidney to the bladder) which was associated with a cancerous change in the adjacent tissues. Elizabeth endured a continuous ache whose origin she could not fathom. I feel the doctors were well advised at this stage in refraining both from revealing to her the proper diagnosis and from using anti-cancer chemotherapy (the tumour was clearly outside the range of surgery, and Elizabeth was eighty-two years old at this time, though remarkably youthful for her age). And so she was treated with painkilling drugs, and laxatives to keep her bowels open. It was pathetic to witness her slow decline both in energy and in physical stature. But she carried on courageously in her house until the help of nurses became essential. Throughout all this time I never let a day go by without telephoning her if I could not visit her. As the malady progressed it became obvious that she found my visits increasingly fatiguing, particularly as she always wanted to give me something to eat if at all possible. Sometimes she spent a few days with her family in the country, but this also became increasingly exhausting, and towards the end of the ordeal she was glad to remain quiet in her own home, quite often in her bed. This account of the lethal progress of cancer is distressingly common, but the redeeming feature was Elizabeth's widening of spiritual awareness and her progressive detachment from all material possessions, even, to a certain extent, human ties.

It was of interest that on the few occasions when she seemed to want the laying-on of hands, I felt a strong resistance on her part, and was not surprised that there was no result other than some temporary relief of her pain, which was becoming increasingly severe as the disease progressed and was barely held in check by the analgesics (painkilling drugs) that were prescribed for her. She was a very independent person who did not relish too much help from outside. Above all, she feared imposing on the resources of those around her. She dreaded becoming a burden on her loving family, and was mercifully able to remain in her own home until she was in too great pain to carry on alone. After her final admission to hospital, an exploratory operation was performed in order to ensure that nothing further could be done in the area of disease to relieve the pain. At this stage the true diagnosis was revealed to her, and concerted steps were taken to relieve the pain without dulling her faculties.

It is always good for a dying person to enter the final phase of life in awareness both of the past that has to be confronted in acceptance and forgiveness and the future whose advent can be greeted with suffused joy. An atmospheric radiance lit up our times together in hospital; all traces of Elizabeth's previous apprehension (based on an inevitable clinging to earthly things) had evaporated, and we could talk about current matters in a lucid delight stemming from a heightened awareness of reality that sees the present as the true focus of eternity. She lost consciousness only during the last few hours of her earthly life, and her body seemed to be transfigured in austere beauty as it entered the end of its allotted span. Even at the end Elizabeth was a great support to her family as well

92

as a source of inspiration to the nurses who attended her. Her final illness dragged on for nearly two years, but the growth in spiritual awareness during that time seemed almost to have justified the suffering she bore with uncomplaining fortitude. Certainly all traces of possessiveness had been washed away as she entered the new life ahead of her. It was a solemn joy to officiate at Elizabeth's funeral service, attended by so many loving friends and relatives. There was an aura of calm release around the bier as it lay in state in the central aisle of the church. The subsequent cremation seemed to complete the soul's liberation.

The third instance of a healing death was that of Frances, another parishioner, who lived some distance from the church but found herself very much at home with our worship. She was elderly, a lovely person whose fine appearance belied her years, and who had had a distinguished record of social service. She had contended for a long time with recurrent cancer of the bladder, for which repeated treatment had been necessary. The pain and social embarrassment of this condition, with its frequent calls to pass urine, had left little trace on her composed face. At last she was ready for the final removal of her bladder and its replacement by an artificial one, tended by a leading urologist while being supported by the prayers of many friends. It was at this stage that I really became involved in the drama, seeing her at her delightful home frequently before and after she had left hospital. The operation itself was a technical success, and soon she was going about her activities with much more energy than for a long time previously. This happy state of affairs did not last long: she developed symptoms of secondary deposits of cancer in the liver which, rather unusually, showed themselves in exhausting attacks of fever. She was very disappointed but not at all disheartened. Though thinner and feebler than before, she was as delighted as ever to see me. Indeed, our times together were so agreeable and our concerns ranged over so many topics that each visit seemed a pleasant social occasion rather than one tinged with more serious business. But we ended with healing and prayer for others in special need. The silence brought us down to the gravity of the situation, but I always left her home with a feeling of uplift in the face of the desperate state of affairs.

All this was, of course, an unspoken tribute to Frances's calm imperturbability which could reach beyond the increasing turmoil of urgency to touch the eternity of the present moment where God is known. In the presence of truly great souls one receives ever so much more than anything one may set out to give; a relationship is born that is not dependent on results or the acclaim of others but exists entirely in its own right. With her usual courage, Frances, in the company of a close friend, went on a fortnight's holiday to France where she died unexpectedly about a week after arrival. And so she was able to avoid the discomfort of terminal care in a hospital, and be of as little trouble to her family and friends as possible. I was quite shocked to hear of her death, for while I rejoiced at her unexpected release, I was once again bereft of a newly found friend. There is little that is hidden from either party in the healing ministry that precedes death.

A number of thoughts arise in relation to these three case-histories: how little effect my ministry had on the course of the disease, how privileged I was to participate in the final act of a life's drama before the soul proceeds to the next stage of its unfolding, and how great is the healing power of death itself, both for the afflicted person and the mourning friends. The work I did in all three instances was simply to be available to give what support I could. My ministry, compared with that of the specialized medical agencies in charge of the patients, was trifling, virtually negligible. I was, as it were, holding their hands as do parents their children's in a moment of pain while the specialists were busy treating diseased tissues and administering potent drugs to relieve suffering. But even had their specialized expertise eradicated the cancer so completely that a full cure followed, I would still have been content with my secondary role. While the specialists contended with the disease, I acted as a channel of power to renew their patients, to strengthen them for the great contests lying immediately ahead of them. For we are more than mere bodies, marvellous as the physical body is in its construction and its built-in mechanisms of maintenance and repair.

To be in a close relationship with a fellow-human is always a privilege, something that friends, let alone close relations, do not appreciate fully until the time of parting. As a minister of healing I have learned to be non-attached to both the person and the results of my service, so that God can work best through me as an unobstructed channel or an untarnished instrument, depending on the particular metaphor one prefers. The greater the degree of non-attachment (a term I prefer to detachment, which seems too clinical and impersonal for any living relationship to emerge), the greater the commitment. On the surface this seems paradoxical, but in fact until one's sight is firmly fixed on God and his service, one's emotions will tend to dominate one's work: when all goes well, the commitment may be one of heavily oppressive solicitude, but when the relationship falters, the commitment may fly out of the window. One's mind goes back to the devotion of Jesus' disciples during the time of his triumphant ministry, and their flight from him when he apparently failed. They learned more about themselves during the period of his passion and death than they did in their three previous years' breathtaking apprenticeship to him.

The joy of a deathbed ministry is that of being able both to guide and to reassure the dying one and to be guided in turn by him or her into realms of experience seldom broached in worldly company. Hospital visiting is a special skill that is seldom appreciated until the visitors have themselves been on the receiving end of the calls. Both Elizabeth and Frances were sometimes exhausted by their visitors, as was I also in my incomparably less serious stay in hospital when Elizabeth proved of such inestimable help. Apart from those few people who possess a genuine healing gift, from whom the warmth of God radiates in love to all around them, most visitors deplete the sick in bed whether at home or in hospital. Therefore one should above all not overstay one's visit. This applies even to close friends and relatives, no matter how devoted they may be and how concerned they feel. A person in bed is a sitting target for all negative feelings that may well up, sometimes unconsciously, from those around him.

In my own illness Elizabeth was the only visitor who filled me with encouragement because she was uncomplicated, of warm heart, and always open to new experiences. Most of the others depressed me, but none more than those who sincerely believed they were spiritually advanced or had a healing gift. I learned so much from that dreadful experience that, as a result, my future healing-counselling ministry became very much wiser and more discerning. An astringency that was foreign to my previous ministry now revealed itself, much, I believe, to the value of those I was subsequently to tend, for now I could speak the truth with less inhibition when candour was desperately required. In hospital visiting the two pitfalls especially to be avoided are a depressed attitude and a tendency to speak too much. Quite a few visitors spend the time getting their own problems off their chests while using the sick person as a captive audience. It would be good if all hospital visitors could spend a few minutes alone in silence before they saw their sick friend, and then made a quiet departure after, at the most, ten minutes. If this were too short a stay, the patient would soon urge a visitor to remain longer, by showing obvious disappointment at the visitor's imminent departure.

Jesus, as we know from the Parable of the Sheep and the Goats (Matthew 25:31–46), enjoins us to help the sick and visit those in prison. Therefore work of this type is our duty as well as our privilege. The question we always have to ask ourselves, however, is: 'Am I doing it because I ought to or because I want to?' It is only when the two coincide that good will come out of the visit. Too much desire exhausts the one who is visited, while too much duty puts the patient in the invidious position of seeming to impose on the visitor's time. If we truly have the well-being of another person at heart, we will neither neglect him nor overwhelm him with our presence. This is the way in which we learn the secret of love, the love that God expends unceasingly upon us. Love enables the person to grow at his own pace into something of the fullness of being that is seen in the saints of the world.

It never leaves us without strength, but it does not impose its strength upon us.

Death the healer is a theme seldom touched on by those still alive in the flesh, yet in the midst of life we are in death. Our stay in this world is necessarily a transient one, and thankfully so, too, once we have completed the particular task we came to perform. In the instance of my three friends, each had fulfilled her life – none was especially distinguished in the world's eyes, nor had any of them that degree of sanctity recorded in the world's annals of the blessed ones, but they all had grown as persons and left much love behind them (more than they could have guessed from their earthly vantage point). Teresa was in her early sixties, Frances and Elizabeth fifteen and twenty years older respectively. But what about the young who die prematurely? If they too have undergone the type of testing I have described with reference to my three friends, they also have done what they were born to achieve even if their lives were cut short before they could have attained worldly eminence. 'The good man, even if he dies an untimely death, will be at rest. For it is not length of life and number of years which bring the honour due to age; if men have understanding, they have grey hairs enough, and an unspotted life is the true ripeness of age' (Wisdom 4:7–9).

Despite the apprehension that progressive, ultimately fatal disease brings to its victims, I am convinced that they have something here that is out of all proportion, in ultimate value, to the suffering they must necessarily undergo in the short term. While everything possible should be done to relieve their distress, the experience of transition is good for the soul, for the essence that is to continue after the outer vestment, the physical body, has been shed. While euthanasia in the context of directly killing an incurably ill person cannot be morally, let alone legally, countenanced because of the abuse that would follow such a course of action if it became generally accepted, there comes a time when the inevitable course of nature towards death need not be strenuously resisted. Here compassion, common sense, and a tacit agreement among the various parties concerned would guide the way. Prayer would be an initiator of action. The ministry of healing has one of its greatest works to fulfil in this field, not least in releasing the soul from attachment to the weary body that is due for dissolution.

9

Maturity and Healing

'Men must endure their going hence, even as their coming hither: ripeness is all,' wrote Shakespeare in *King Lear*. That ripeness is the measure of one's maturity. Like a fruit fit to be eaten, so is a mature person fit for the next stage in the unceasing pageant of life that transcends all phases of transition that we call death. In the three vignettes of dying people that we considered in the previous chapter, maturity was seen to come to its fullness as the sufferers contended courageously with their drawn-out final adversity, and then they were ready for their next commission. My mind goes back to the Nunc Dimittis, where the aged Simeon calls to God for his discharge in peace now that he has seen with his own eyes the living Christ, the deliverance prepared in full view of the world to enlighten the heathen and to be the ultimate glory of the Jews – both of whom up to the present have either ignored him or else categorically rejected him. And yet our Lord lives in the hearts of all people as a seed of conscience, and will never cease to make his presence known until germinated in each one of us and grown in stature to the full tree of life. In him alone is the way to the abundant life, the life of complete, fulfilled healing in which every aberrant element has been restored to its place in the pattern of a fully alive person.

Maturation is a process, and maturity is not so much an end-point as a climate of existence in which the person can emanate his unique essence to the world in tranquil joy while

he imbibes the essence of all the world around him. In giving
we receive more of the Spirit of God; in receiving we draw
an unending stream of life to us, so that we in turn can
contribute even more of ourselves to the demanding thirst of
the wider community. Having nothing to fear, since God is
active within us as a germinating seed, we can respond positively to those who would know more about the life of
completeness. We now have nothing of our own while
possessing all things in their own fullness. What we cling to
acts as a blockage preventing us from being available to the
full challenge of present experience; finally we have to be so
full of our own integrity that we become the little child who
alone, in the words of Christ, can enter the Kingdom of God.

Even Mary of Magdala was told by the risen Christ not to
cling to him, not to touch him any more, for he had not yet
ascended to the Father. Jesus himself can all too easily become
an idol to worship from afar rather than an ever-present
reality to know as we grow closer to him in our own lives.
And yet the very presence of Christ within is the impetus
of personal growth. In maturity he permeates our unique
personalities, making them even more radiant and individual
as we are transformed into his likeness. The name is ours but
the presence is his. The mature person has fulfilled his life
on earth. To be sure, he has not attained perfection – the
greatest saints know of their unworthiness – but he has
completed a phase of his growth into full personhood. Even
our weaknesses are illuminated by a divine love so that they
too are part of his glory. Above all, we can forgive wholeheartedly even as we are humble enough to seek and receive
forgiveness both from God and from our fellow-creatures
struggling on the path of life.

One person I know well is striving towards maturity within
a stunted personality, and his story is worth close attention.
His background was appalling; his parents had little love for
him, while his brother was the favourite. He was regarded as
merely second-rate, and when he grew up he was fortunate
to attain a minor clerical post. He had an ear for music and
was quite a skilful performer on the piano and later on the
organ also. He was obsessed by one theme only – his failure

in the theatre of worldly affairs. And so he tried, precariously placed as he was, to assert himself. To this end he contracted a marriage that turned out disastrously. His wife had severe personality problems of her own, but her condition was not helped by her emotionally damaged, inadequate husband, who now had the guilt of a divorce added to the burden of impotence and failure he had been accustomed to bear for so many years. It was in this state of despair, as a man in later middle age with little apparent future, that he first came to me. I in fact did little more than minister to his dereliction in the solicitude of undiverted awareness. He was at this time in the process of moving in the direction of his native Christian faith that he had previously rejected, and we talked around various biblical passages that had in them the seeds of contemplative silence. He also was able to bring his meaningless existence to the surface, and see the positive aspects of the paroxysms of anger that so disrupted his private life.

In my experience most situations of blind fury have a background of fear which has to be acknowledged and confronted. Once the fear is lightened by the counsellor's instructed compassion – and this is a real commodity only when the counsellor has come to terms with the mosaic structure of light and darkness which is his own psyche – love can make its quiet, unhurried entry into the souls of all those involved in the situation, and slowly the fear is illuminated by that love. Fear is, in the end, related to self-preservation, and on one level is an innate mechanism of defence that keeps the body alive: without it we would endanger ourselves recklessly day by day. One has to be in dire straits before one seriously considers the self-annihilation implicit in suicide – if, indeed, any significant part of the personality other than its encompassing physical body is destroyed at the event of death.

On a more psychic level of existence we are threatened continually by those who seem to be more powerful than we ourselves, whether in matters of material success, interpersonal relationships or spiritual authority; if we do not take a definite stand we feel we could easily be taken over by various powerful personalities, armed with an arrogant self-esteem, who would ride roughshod over all that resists them. We yearn for their defeat and deflation. However, in the end, if we cannot defend ourselves by the strength within us, we will react by projecting our hatred on to convenient scapegoats who can be identified with the manifold groups around us that, by their success, impress us with our own inferiority. The person at peace in himself is most unlikely to feel threatened inwardly; or, as Jesus would put it, if our house is built on rock it will withstand the onslaught of the elements of the weather, but if the foundation is merely sand the house will soon collapse to the ground. The analogy is especially helpful when we recall that God is frequently identified as the Rock of Israel in the Psalms, while in 1 Corinthians 10:4 St Paul extends the analogy to Christ himself.

To return to the person I was describing earlier: as love gradually warmed his heart by a conscious presence and not merely a spiritual injunction, so he began to open out more to those around him. He performed simple acts of kindness such as reading to a blind man and helping patients in hospital. In due course he tremblingly embarked on a second marriage, this time to a woman some years his senior, whose presence eased the way of his unfolding to a more adult state of mind. Her love for him was genuine, proved by her support for his faltering steps. She acted as the Bible portrays God's providence in Isaiah 40:29–31: giving strength to the wearied and powerless even in excess of the overflowing vitality of the young; these may tire, but fatigue does not touch those infused by God's presence in their lives.

He gave music lessons and played the organ at his church, thereby also becoming more integrated into the congregation. At the same time he became reconciled to his more prosperous brother without, however, striking any great depth of loving-kindness in the restored relationship. This takes a long time to achieve, and is, like all other experiences of conversion, a pure gift of God, his grace that suffices in our daily work. The reconciliation was the outer evidence of his conversion, whose end will, I believe, be gloriously effected in the life ahead of him. This is true for us as we quit the mortal body and assume our spiritual vesture, as pure ultimately as the white gown worn by the redeemed sinner who is then the bride of Christ.

The sense of lonely frustration is still very much a part of this man's character. Recently his wife's health has deteriorated so severely that she needs constant assistance. This has in its turn drawn out of him a sense of responsibility that would at one time have been inconceivable: he now has to make decisions on his own, dogged as he is by the constant fear of bereavement and the loneliness that will follow in its wake. I have assured him not only of my own support but also of the friendship that will be extended him by the many people he has befriended on his slow, tortured path towards completion. Time will show how well he can cope with the difficulties ahead of him, but there is little doubt that the healing relationship between us has provided the impetus for an expansion in his awareness of the things that really matter in life and the way towards their attainment.

To me the finest example of maturation in the Bible is the life of the prophet Jeremiah. Though chosen even before his conception in the womb to be God's special mouthpiece to the recalcitrant Israelites, his forthright denunciations of the corrupt régime estranged him more and more from the people around him, even his close relatives. His life became increasingly restricted because of the vicious hostility his honesty evoked, and he bemoaned his fate, even cursing the day of his birth (as did also Job, possibly a fictional reconstruction of the character of the earlier prophet). However, God gave him no material support whatsoever apart from seeing that his life was preserved. Indeed, the Almighty on one occasion told him to stop grumbling and proceed with the work, otherwise he would select another more obedient prophet. In fact, when one is under the driving power of the Holy Spirit one can no more desist from doing God's work than one can voluntarily hold one's breath to the extremity of being asphyxiated. As the prophet matured, so his ministry became calmer, even though his suffering, if anything, increased in intensity. He accepted the obvious fact that he was under divine commission, and learned to trust even in situations of terror that would seem logically to have had within them the seeds of total destruction. Death is in any case the inevitable end of all mortal life, but we can at least enter its portals with nobility. It was this that Jeremiah was learning; the mature person can face whatever the future holds with equanimity, a calm acceptance suffused with joy.

The peak of Jeremiah's prophetic ministry was reached in his proclamation of the new covenant God was to make with his people Israel: an interior spirituality superseding if not eclipsing outer religious instruction, as the heart becomes the place of divine meeting (31:31–34). With the Law deeply implanted within them, they will at last learn to do good, which is essentially the same as knowing the divine presence as an intimate friend. In the face of such a prophecy all worldly rewards pale into insignificance: the work for the Kingdom is its own reward, for it brings that Kingdom into the place of immediate concern. Time and eternity intersect at the point of the present moment. We may with confidence sense the inner freedom enjoyed by Jeremiah even when he was carried off to Egypt by a rebellious band of his own people. The body remained rooted in the earth, but the soul ascended to the world of the immortals. It is of interest that Jeremiah's reputation rose high in the esteem of later generations so that in the Maccabaean period he ranked as a protecting saint of the people (2 Maccabees 15:13–16).

Another of the people to whom I ministered was Deirdre, a woman afflicted from her youth with severe diabetes that was later complicated by progressive affection of the blood vessels. She had one leg amputated because of gangrene, her sight was impaired, and the diabetes itself was hard to control even under strict supervision. Though she was in her middle years when I knew her, she had a fairylike youthfulness about her and she carried on her work remarkably well as a physiotherapist. It was always a joy to be with her because of her unself-conscious outlook and freedom from obvious resentment at the cruel blow that providence had dealt her. It was in the 1960s that I first met her, and she was sympathetic to the 'new age' metaphysical outlook which was very prominent at that time. This is in fact a paganism brought up to date with gnostic accretions culled from psychic sources and heavily flavoured by theosophical speculations derived from unorthodox offshoots of the world's major religious traditions. It is still the current esotericism, and is liberating in the generous sweep of its sympathies, but it fails very often in its inability to discern facts from fiction, acknowledged truth from individualistic opinion. It shares with its theological adversary, the Renewal Movement, a confidence in its own sources of inspiration and an enthusiasm for miraculous healings and other spectacular phenomena which can then be enlisted as proof of higher forms of intelligence directing the course of human destiny.

Whereas Renewal trusts implicitly in what it regards as the working of the Holy Spirit and the power of Christ (the Father is often bypassed in Charismatic enthusiasm), the New Age Movement puts its trust in vast cosmic powers, spiritual 'masters' and lesser 'teachers', all emanating from exalted sources in the intermediate psychic sphere. It tends to dismiss traditional Christianity as out of date, confidently assured of having a more enlightened view of 'The Christ', who seems to be identified even more with an enhanced consciousness of reality than with a personal presence (considered a 'master', one among others). Both Renewal and New Age conferences are often stunning in their exuberant fellowship and faith, but both approaches again tend to be less impressive when the darkness of human tragedy descends like the dusk after a sunny day. Each is in fact a witness of aspects of truth, particularly in what it affirms; in their dogmatic denials lies their inadequacy. Both traffic in psychic phenomena which are morally neutral. What matters in the end is the emergence of a new individual modelled on the person of Jesus Christ. This is the measure of a real healing, though, of course, our sights have to be lowered to what is practicable in our world of ambivalent values and destructive discord, lest we give up in despair even before we start the great work of transmutation.

It has to be admitted that the Christian faith is often presented with a narrow-minded intolerance and a discouragingly negative regard for human nature as hopelessly rooted in sin. While this view is not without its truth, when it is pressed to an extreme position it tends to encourage an attitude of guilt and fear, seldom far below the surface of consciousness even at the best of times. This spoils the natural pleasures that God has prepared for our enjoyment. As a result the flow of the life-giving Holy Spirit is sadly quenched. It is no wonder that many seekers who find the Christian way inhibiting, even in its Charismatic exuberance, have embraced the New Age life-style. This tends to dispense with sin as it views the world through rose-tinted spectacles of blissful credulity, while averting its gaze from the jarring contrasts of light and darkness that are the very bases of human existence. If Renewal lays too much stress on the battle against demonic agencies to the point of cutting itself off from large areas of human experience, the New Age consciousness is so open that it is liable to swallow any new idea as a fresh revelation of cosmic truth. In fact, to the person using his innate spiritual intuition, both these ways, even when bathed in the light of fellowship, are suffused with an underlying darkness that evokes deeper misgivings.

It must be said that not every 'word of knowledge' uttered in a Renewal meeting is of the Holy Spirit, nor are all New Age 'messages' to be accepted as coming from trustworthy sources. Illusion creeps in, especially when we are sure of ourselves, handing over our intellectual discrimination and intuitive awareness in blind trust to an external source of spiritual direction, even if that source claims divine authority. Both ways have their individual use in bringing the agnostic seeker or the conventional worshipper, as the case may be, to a realm of experience far beyond that of the unimaginative world in which he pursues the common round of existence. But the spiritual path soon leads beyond these approaches to a deeper, more silent communion with God. In him alone do all the antitheses coinhere, for the divine wisdom can take within itself both the linear truth of the scientist and the holistic understanding of the mystic. In God the peaks of pagan awe can be illuminated by the simple love of Christ. There is no question of the one approach eliminating the other. On the contrary, each gives of its genius to the whole, and in so doing effects its transmutation to divine essence.

Deirdre herself attended as many conferences on the 'new consciousness' as her physical condition would permit. Her Christian background was pushed even further aside in the wake of fascinating New Age teachings. She continued gallantly as a physiotherapist, even when her health was at a lower ebb than that of many of her patients. She sent me a number of people for help, one of whom was amazingly guided through a severe psychic brainstorm to a healing maturity that continues to this day. Another was a beautiful young married woman, a medical practitioner suffering from cancer, whom I was privileged to tend up to the time of her death some months later. But with Deirdre I had a deep, though distant, relationship that lasted for many years. Her diabetic condition deteriorated, as is the rule when the blood vessels are severely affected by the disease. As the body failed, so the soul rose in glory. She ceased to be attached to the nebulous psychic realm, and practised an inner silence that brought her close to God. She radiated a peace that no longer depended on the assurance given by mediums or esoteric teachers, useful as both may be to seekers on the lower rungs of the ladder of self-knowledge. The same note of caution is necessary in respect of regular attendance at church services, as a way of spiritual growth, if there is not a burning desire for self-transcendence in the heart of the worshipper. The very Body and Blood of Christ may be consumed, but the will is necessary before the elements of the Eucharist can start to heal a diseased body or a broken mind.

I remember especially vividly my last visit to Deirdre in hospital. Her kidneys were failing, a common event in the terminal stages of diabetes, and she knew, far more precisely than I, that her end was in sight. She was concerned only about my welfare, that I had travelled some distance to see her and that I looked tired. She was full of concern also for her fellow-patients in the long ward, strangely a place of peaceful sharing despite the busy nursing routines with their inevitable clamour. Though she had moved far away from the traditional Christian faith of the denomination into which she was born, she found the Eucharist a comfort, and was a living representative of the Lord, so often concealed rather than revealed by the insensitive and the intolerant. At the end I gave her the laying-on of hands followed by a blessing, and we then remained together in silence for some minutes. Despite the open character of the ward, my private ministration evoked no comment; probably the others present were so engrossed in their own affairs that they did not so much as take in what we two were doing. I purposely refrained from wanting the curtains around Deirdre's bed to be drawn, since I was a visitor and not an attending doctor or nurse; my role was that of a minister of healing and not a medical practitioner. After the silence we took leave of one another, and a celestial radiance emanated from Deirdre. As I walked along the outer corridor, I was assailed by the stench of urine and faeces coming from an adjacent sluice room where bedpans and urinals were emptied and rinsed. The contrast between this and the heavenly peace around Deirdre showed me how necessary it was to bring that unearthly beauty right down to earth, as Deirdre had done in her own way when she was still active both as a physiotherapist and a vibrant individual.

One of the sure hallmarks of the maturing process is a growing insight into one's own character with special reference to previous blind spots and glaring faults – these are of a different order to the endearing foibles that are part of oneself. I have known people of high professional attainment blissfully unaware of the havoc they were wreaking upon their associates because of their selfishness and inability to respect other members of their profession as individuals in their own right. Quite a number of such disruptive people have high moral principles and sincere religious convictions. There are yet other individuals who are steeped in a spiritual tradition, yet who behave with crass insensitivity to a friend in sore need of rest and quietness. Maturity and nobility of character in fact proceed hand in hand. The naturally self-aware person who can project himself into the personality of his neighbour is a spiritual aristocrat whatever his religious belief; in his sensitive, caring attention he brings the power of God to whomsoever he meets in the course of his labours. Being integrated around the centre of God in his personality, he becomes the vehicle of the Holy Spirit. One can read spiritual classics without ceasing, but until one leaves them for a time and, instead, offers oneself without reserve to God in the moment in hand, one will remain outside the Kingdom, groping for the doorkey while the whole cosmos lies open for inspection and participation.

Maturity can also lead to a widening of spiritual perspective. One of my dearest friends, Stephen, was a priest in the Catholic tradition of the Anglican Church. Its ritual was the staple of his existence. He defended Catholic principles to the bitter end, on one memorable occasion striving to install the Reserved Sacrament in a church with a much more Protestant tradition. The conflict ended in a court case and he was, not surprisingly, the loser. The outcome nearly destroyed him. When we first met he was a widower of some years' duration; his wife had been seven years older than he, and they were childless. We met through the introduction of an osteopath who was treating him for a painful back. As is not unusual with practitioners of alternative medicine, her sympathies, basically Christian, extended liberally to other avenues of thought, and she felt, having heard me speak at a conference on the interaction of faith and healing, that I could be of some assistance in opening Stephen's vision to a larger vista of reality than was contained in the rather narrow confines of his concerns. She little guessed the important role she was destined to play in both our lives.

I found that Stephen radiated love. He was at that time chaplain to a women's religious community, all of whose members were well advanced in age. His ministry extended to other convents in the region where he functioned as confessor and spiritual adviser. I have met no other man who could form so beautifully chaste a relationship with so many different types of women. At that time I was starting to emerge from my own shell of reserve, and I found we could relate to one another at once in the closest harmony despite the broad, undogmatic scope of my own spiritual sympathies. His personality as well as his words made the Catholic faith the ultimate truth to me, a stance that remains my own to this day. But I, almost as a fool in comparison with his own background, broadened his vision at the same time, not only by my innately freer relationship with God, but also by introducing him to classics from other spiritual traditions. A book I have long especially valued is Sarvepalli Radhakrishnan's translation of the *Bhagavadgita*, with his memorable commentary on its verses. He was at one time Spalding Professor of Eastern Religion and Ethics at Oxford and later became President of India. Stephen, too, found many good things in this book, the product of a truly catholic Hindu mind, and encountered little in its depth at variance with the heart of the Catholic faith by which he ordered his life. Of course, the theological stance of this great classic of Hinduism differs considerably from the Christian revelation, especially in its treatment of human destiny and the place of Jesus Christ in the salvation of the world. (The Hindu would see Jesus as one avatar – a descent of the Divine into the human frame – among an assembly of other great world teachers, rather than as the unique Son of God proclaimed in the Christian faith.) But the deeper truth of spiritual life, the 'perennial philosophy' as Leibniz called it, is one and the same. In Aldous Huxley's book of the same name, he defined the 'perennial philosophy' as 'the metaphysic that recognizes a divine Reality substantial to the world of things and lives and minds; the psychology that finds in the soul something similar to, or even identical with, divine Reality; the ethic that places man's final end in the knowledge of the immanent and transcendent Ground of all being – the thing is immemorial and universal'.

Stephen was the one who arranged my final reception into the Anglican Church on Easter Eve 1971. We both knew intuitively that this was a preliminary to priesthood within the denomination's broad domain – he with pleasant anticipation, I with mounting apprehension, as I felt that such a ministry would both cut me off from my wide spiritual roots and separate me from many of my professional colleagues in the medical field. A year after this, I preached my first Good Friday addresses from the pulpit of the convent chapel, a meditation on Jesus' seven 'last words' from the cross, starting at noon and ending three hours later. Not a year has gone by since then without my preaching this most moving meditation on the day that commemorates Christ's final identification with the pain of the world and his transcendence of it by sheer love. Only as the Holy Spirit inspires one in the course of preaching the service does one begin to participate in the reconciliation of the world to God effected by that life, cut short so terribly by agonizing pain and then resurrected to full glory in God's power.

Stephen was privileged to know that agony in the course of his own life soon after I had preached in his chapel. He had had a severe heart attack, and at the same time the aorta (the large artery that leads off from the heart to the back of the trunk, supplying branches to the whole of the lower part of the body) became weakened and dilated almost to the point of rupture. This 'aneurysm', as it is called, should be repaired as soon as possible, for otherwise it may either burst and lead to rapid death by sheer blood loss, or else it may press on vital structures and interfere with their function. Stephen was in constant pain, and his helpless weakness was in stark contrast to his former strength of voice that issued forth so beautifully as he sang at the Eucharist and the daily Office. I consulted him on one occasion about the Holy Spirit, who was to be the theme of a retreat I was soon to conduct. All he could do in his extremity was to point me to the great Russian Orthodox saint Seraphim of Sarov, from whom that same Spirit issued forth as a dazzlingly radiant presence when he prayed to God that a certain disciple should see the Spirit directly. This episode is recorded in *The Mystical Theology of the Eastern Church*, by Vladimir Lossky. Yes indeed, the Holy Spirit is known and shown in our own lives, and he speaks, not on his own authority, but as a guide into the whole truth, imparting all that he hears and leading us to the full knowledge of God's glory as revealed in Christ (John 16:13–15). We do not define the Spirit so much as be unceasingly informed by his presence, as he leads us into vaster areas of truth such as we are able to comprehend in our own state of spiritual progress.

The operation for the repair of the aneurysm of Stephen's abdominal aorta was postponed at the last moment, an unfortunate hitch that completely undermined his confidence –

how often do medical staff cavalierly alter arrangements without so much as a moment's thought about their patients' psychological state! When he was readmitted to hospital a month later, he was at a very low ebb, and I was not surprised that he failed to rally after the aortic repair. I visited him the day before he died – he was inarticulate, but his profound distress was very obvious. He died after a further heart attack, a passing as bleak as that of Jesus himself.

The greater glory was his, however, when his body lay in state in the chapel he had served so well, and the crowds of mourners paid their last respects before his interment alongside his wife. He, too, had experienced a resurrection from a restricted view of Christ to a greater revelation of the divine splendour. This splendour was poured out in the love of all those who mourned him: not a single relative that I can remember, but numerous close friends from all walks of life. It was sad that he died before I was ordained deacon and then priest, the latter event taking place four and a half years after I had been received into the Church (on the Feast of St Matthew, 21 September 1975). But he stood with me at the threshold of a ministry that has been the final seal on a friendship which thrives now as strongly as it did when he was last alive with me in the flesh some sixteen years ago. He is with me each afternoon when I remember my deceased friends in prayer.

10

The Ministry of Love

All real ministry is love, the spontaneous outpouring of oneself
in deepest concern for the other person without thought of
reward other than seeing that person relieved of his burden.
The result is the reward, but so also is the action even where
there is no obvious outcome that could in any way be seen
as favourable. Since God is love, we start to love by being
open to that love in awareness of the present moment, the
instant when the divine compassion touches our hearts and
brings us to full consciousness of the pain around us. It follows
therefore that two prerequisites of knowing and showing love
are awareness and sensitivity. In turn it comes about that we
have first to be aware of ourselves as living creatures and
sensitive to the turgid stream of emotions continually coursing
through us as the events of the moment make their presence
felt. It is no wonder that the golden rule expounded in one
form or another in all the world's manifold spiritual traditions
is, 'Always treat others as you would like them to treat you'.
This injunction from Matthew 7:12 adds that the whole
teaching of the Law and the Prophets points to this ultimate
state of loving relationship. Elsewhere St Paul reminds us
that love cannot wrong a neighbour, therefore the whole Law
is summed up in love (Romans 13:10).

Love frequently begins as a scarcely rational emotional
attraction to another person: it demands recognition and will
never stay content until it has achieved its end. When indeed

this end has been achieved, it may be found less attractive than was envisaged: we, as it were, fell in love with an illusion magnified out of all proportion by the need of our own condition. The proof of love is to continue the caring even when disillusion has stripped the glamour from the object of our devotion. It requires strict honesty – the refusal to evade the facts of our own reactions however negative they may be – and yet to proceed in faith, seeing by the grace of God something lovable even in our moments of deepest doubt when we feel that nothing profitable can come out of the situation. As we persist in faith, so the scales of illusion drop off our own inner eyes, and we begin to see the person in his true light – a brother striving as oneself for a place in the light of God's presence. When we have attained this understanding, which is an amalgam of divine grace and personal commitment, we have somehow come to terms with our own deepest problems and can relax with relieved humour in our own situation. In fact, we are now fully open to the love of God which pours with gathering strength onto the beloved, and also onto an increasing range of people in our vicinity. Love that is real, in other words, cannot be restricted to individuals in isolation, but finds its level in a universal outgiving that excludes no one from its concern. When we know this love in that fullness, we are experiencing healing, and are able to be a focus of healing for a body of people of diverse beliefs and life-styles, whose one burning desire is to stay alive and work according to their abilities.

In an aspiring life, one that is climbing the perilous ledges of the spiritual mountain – something of the Mount Carmel that St John of the Cross described – a few special people stand out clearly as kindred souls on the path of proficiency. Such has been Freda in my own life. I met her originally at Mary Macaulay's Centre where she acted as an unpaid assistant – indeed, money was so sparse apart from a meagre – soon to be withdrawn – grant from the London County Council of those days, that all of us acted purely out of concern for the vision of the founder without thought for our own resources. In fact, the gain was out of all proportion to any pecuniary reward: it produced friendships of an order deeper than any I have ever since encountered. Freda was thirty years older than I, but at once a harmony was struck between us that had the character of a preordained relationship. We both had an inner stillness that could unite more strongly than any exchange of words, even if we might disagree about a particular matter on a superficial intellectual level. A dedicated meditation group, set up by Freda, soon flourished among a core of us. There were no esoteric teachings or specialized techniques, only the hush of a silence of deep caring fellowship in which we were all open to the divine spark within us, a spark that is of the same nature as the Holy Spirit himself. The aim of the group was to assist the work of the Centre by inner prayer, since Mary Macaulay herself was an activist rather than a contemplative by disposition, but soon our intercessions were more widely based and indeed bore an amazing fruit of healings at a distance for people none of us had ever met.

On one occasion a psychic member of the group claimed contact with a deceased soul, but this rather jarred with our work and was not encouraged. Indeed, the silence itself brings a conviction of the soul's immortality, but the experience is one of pure grace. We in turn have to be ready to receive it, hence the urgency for meditation groups like ours, provided the spur is loving service rather than selfish indulgence. We started with a spiritual reading, usually biblical, or a piece of music, and then the radiant silence poured down on us like a benediction from on high. The silence of God has a love about it that distinguishes it from all mere meditation exercises; it is warm and welcoming, reminding us of Jesus' invitation, 'Come to me, all whose work is hard, whose load is heavy; and I will give you relief' (Matthew 11:28). This seems to be the heart of Christian contemplation, even if some of the members of the group may profess an agnosticism that precludes religious commitment.

Freda's background was a deeply tragic one: her beloved daughter had died of asthma while still a child, and her husband, a weak, emotionally unbalanced man who needed constant adulation, had ultimately committed suicide in the face of mounting charges of embezzlement of funds. She sustained severe internal injuries during the Second World War, which necessitated major abdominal surgery and the removal of most of her stomach. As a result of this her digestion was impaired, and the nourishment necessary for her survival was provided mostly by meat – in fact, I have already alluded to her need in connexion with diet, health and spirituality. As a result of her digestive problems she was painfully thin: largely a covering of skin with underlying bones, but with a spirit so vibrant that no one in her company could fail to be renewed and restored to hope. Though diet remained an overriding concern, she had never lost her sparkle or sense of humour for any length of time.

Eventually Freda left Mary Macaulay's Centre to help in a new healing home in the country. The proprietress, a woman of independent means with a considerable gift of contact healing, wanted her home to be a place of instruction as well as healing (as if the two can ever be separated!), and Freda arranged for speakers to come for weekend conferences. She also led a group for meditation. I visited the place quite often, and it was then that Freda first told me that she could not see properly; there seemed to be a film over her eyes. At first I did not take much notice of the matter, but the visual deterioration rapidly became serious. She consulted specialists in a world-famous London eye hospital and was given the verdict: she was suffering from a progressive degeneration of the retina (the layer of cells at the back of the eye which is sensitive to light, and relays the information via the optic nerve to the brain, which in turn interprets the message into form and colour), and could look forward to only six months' more useful sight. The cause of the retinal degeneration was undecided, but malnutrition could have played a role in it. She was given large doses of vitamin pills that she could not digest; injections were more easily assimilated, but soon those too became an intolerable burden.

I did what I could with the laying-on of hands (both to the head and around the eyes) and constant prayer, but with an inner assurance that, despite the terrible prognosis, all would be well – or at least as well as could be reasonably hoped. This assurance was certainly not medical, nor was it a pious religious faith; it was a voice within telling me to get on with the work in complete trust, neither looking for results nor trying to prove the efficacy of spiritual healing so as to assert God's over-all providence. The heat that I had felt radiating from Constance Peters' hands about four years previously, when I received the amazing amelioration from the effects of hay fever that I described at the beginning of this book, now radiated from my own hands as I ministered to Freda. Both she and I were aware of the heat in the area of the head. Though beneficial results in other people had followed my ministrations before this work began, I had never previously received a subjective confirmation that something was happening.

Since then the phenomenon has been very frequent; on the other hand, I am exquisitely aware of rejection when a person does not want my service. This seems paradoxical, that a person should seek healing in order simply to reject it, but the solution lies in unconscious (and often conscious) pride which sets itself up to refuse help. The situation was shown in Nazareth, Jesus' home town, when the inhabitants so cut off his spiritual flow by their tacit hostility that he could do virtually nothing there apart from a few minor healings. This particular episode, recorded in Matthew 13:53–58 and Mark 6:1–6, has always been, in my judgement, the proof of Jesus' healing work. Had it been one long story of success, I would have been distinctly sceptical of the accounts of his work and even the reliability of the gospel writers. Failure is so close to everyday experience that, until it is acknowledged, we cannot pass beyond it to success; then at last we can do the work for its sake alone while we get out of the way. The ego is an essential servant but a demonic master. It is for this reason that I flinch from those who give impressive accounts of their healing prowess but sweep the more mundane unsuccessful side under the carpet. True healing is a slow, unobtrusive process which taxes the faith of minister and patient alike. We all have our dramatic cures, but these are not the heart of the matter.

My healing ministry to Freda has continued for twenty-two years: unceasing prayer and regular periods of the laying-on of hands. Her sight outdistanced the dismal forecasts of the specialists, and despite her defective vision, she has been able to lead an independent existence for all this time. A few years after the trouble began, cataracts were removed from both eyes (at that time the modern, remarkably effective lens implantation technique was in its early stage and not generally available in hospital practice). The operations were not without their complications, but she recovered well and was able to use contact lenses for some years, until she found it impossible to insert them properly and was therefore obliged to dispense with them. Nevertheless, useful vision has been retained, and she can still read books of larger print (and of more modest print also, with the aid of a magnifying glass). I would not for one moment claim that my ministrations have been responsible for this wonderful retention of visual acuity – I am well aware through my own training that the prognostications of even the most eminent specialists are only approximate, especially in obscure degenerations affecting the sense organs – but the manner in which Freda's sight has survived the inevitable enfeeblement of the ageing process is most impressive.

Even more important than this amelioration of failing sight has been the close relationship that has developed between us. There are no topics of conversation that we cannot approach without the experience of a deep love, even when disagreeing profoundly about a special issue. Freda's survival into her ninety-third year is remarkable enough, considering her parlous physical condition. It is quite possible that her long-standing emaciation has worked against her early death, since the heart has a lesser burden to bear in very thin individuals. It is well established that overweight people have a diminished life expectancy as well as being particularly prone to osteoarthritis of the weight-bearing joints such as the hips and knees. Old age is often considered to be more a burden than a special blessing of God, despite the encouraging view of longevity we find in the Psalms and the wisdom books of the Old Testament. Freda's longevity has been a blessing to innumerable people even though her inevitable enfeeblement has been a great trial to her. At this stage of her life she would dearly like to make the great transition we call death, but to her chagrin the periods of illness pass by, and she finds herself once more in her dogged, indefatigable, if debilitated, body. It would appear that she still has some work to do among her fellow-residents in the pleasant home for the elderly where she now lives.

And so a healing I was privileged to initiate has borne fruit out of all proportion to what was given. Two new people have emerged – she and I – and with her constant tacit support I have explored without ceasing the ground, the very foundation, of the healing process as I enter into the depths of the spiritual core of all creation. She in her turn, fiercely opposed to all violence, has had to work within the confines of a body in constant revolt and a community so unconcerned with her insights as to be innately hostile to them. As we both move towards our final period of enlightenment (she apparently more imminently than I, thirty years younger but by no means out of range of the violence ahead of us all), we can both thank God for his introduction and our deep witness together. The work is indeed one, for we both function from the level of the soul. No one who touches Freda is quite the same afterwards, for something of life's eternity impinges on that person also. This does not imply that she (or I) does not experience periods of despondency and obscuration of vision, when all spiritual statements seem to be pure wishful thinking if not psychopathological delusions. In this world the dense fog of agnostic scientific thought, naked emotional violence, and corruption in the highest places of society – and sometimes of the universal Church as well – almost completely occludes the rays of divine grace that sustain us all, good and bad alike, in our daily work. To continue in the darkness is the proof of our faith, to persist without bitterness is the measure of our love. In contact with a person of love a cure may not occur, but the wayfarer is strangely strengthened for whatever work lies ahead. He knows where his human supports are to be found, and through them he can proceed beyond their guidance into the light of God.

Love can, alas, be rejected. One of the most painful experiences in my healing work concerns Emily, a woman whom I

119

had supported constantly after the death of her husband Richard, a spiritual colleague of great integrity, as was she also at that time. Richard died at a ripe old age, and his considerably younger widow was virtually friendless apart from the close circle in which her husband had worked, the group where I had first met him. None of the other members of this circle apparently came to Emily's assistance, apart from me – although I must concede with hindsight that they may well have made attempts of caring and been summarily turned away by Emily, who had a tendency to mental instability. I telephoned her regularly, not only to see that she was well but also to establish a firm friendship so that she could call on me in an emergency. And so the relationship continued for about ten years. I often visited her and gave her spiritual healing at the end of a pleasant Sunday afternoon together. She herself had a considerable gift of psychic sensitivity and also of intercessory prayer for the sick. When I moved into my present residence Emily gave me a large amount of her spare furniture and also some very attractive pictures which now adorn the walls of the sitting-room where I do my counselling and healing work. The gift was especially welcome as I had almost exhausted my financial reserves in this hazardous move, done almost as much for the benefit of those who visited me as for my own comfort.

The relationship was easy and relaxed, and we could discuss anything with complete openness. I regarded Emily as one of my really reliable friends whom I would have entrusted with my very life. Her psychic sensitivity was a useful adjunct to my own, and we were able to do some deliverance work together, although at that time this ministry did not figure prominently in my work. In 1982 Emily fell victim to fulminating attacks of asthma which necessitated emergency hospital treatment; breast cancer was also discovered. From that time onwards her friendship with me cooled. She found the healing I gave her to be repellent, and she began to take exception to what I said to her, though in fact my own warm regard for her had not changed, and I telephoned her as frequently as ever. At first I could not believe that anything was seriously wrong, putting her attitude down to the large doses of steroids she had been given for her asthma and the hormone treatment administered for her breast cancer. However, the relationship soon became fraught as she accused me, quite unjustly, of saying something unpleasant to her. I fortunately did not utter a single angry word, since I was dumbfounded by her baseless accusation. Soon afterwards she put the receiver down when I telephoned her, and this rejection, on the Saturday before Palm Sunday in 1983, was the last communication I was destined to have with her. I learned indirectly that she died some three years after our final break, but my prior attempts at a reconciliation by letter received no acknowledgement.

I was shattered by this rejection after so many years of sharing ourselves together, and even today I can come to no entirely rational explanation. The basic mental instability must have been important, as Emily did in the past have occasional delusions of persecution that seemed to fade away in the course of a few months. I could easily attribute her strange behaviour to a combination of mental disturbance, progressive illness and drug therapy. But there may have been deeper psychic invasion, for she was a 'sensitive' with no clear religious commitment. Mediumship is a mixed blessing, to be used with impunity only when the person is totally committed to God in a higher religious faith, preferably the Christian one. As St Paul says in a famous passage, 'Find your strength in the Lord, in his mighty power. Put on all the armour which God provides so that you may be able to stand firm against the devices of the devil. For our fight is not against human foes, but against cosmic powers, against the authorities and potentates of this dark world, against the superhuman forces of evil in the heavens' (Ephesians 6:11–12). Certainly a ministry of love was shattered by unseen forces, but my concern did not cease. Now that death has united Richard and Emily, I include them both in my prayers each afternoon when I remember an increasing number of friends who have made the great transition. I believe that all is well with Emily and me now, as she has been united with her husband and I have moved on to greater work in the unseen dimensions.

The writer of the Song of Songs knew well when he wrote, 'Love is strong as death, passion cruel as the grave; it blazes up like blazing fire, fiercer than any flame. Many waters cannot quench love, no flood can sweep it away; if a man were to offer for love the whole wealth of his house, it would be utterly scorned' (8:6–7). In St Paul's famous rhapsody on love in 1 Corinthians 13, he comes to the heart of the matter at the beginning of the eighth verse, 'Love will never come to an end'. One may have to cease all tangible communication with the recalcitrant beloved, but the heart does not grow cold with neglect or indifference. Like the father who runs out in hysterical joy to welcome the Prodigal Son, so the heart waits in mute expectation for all the world's outcasts to be finally reinstated in the body of humanity. Only then can love show us the way to the unitive knowledge of God which is once again pure love.

The mention of malign invasion of the psyche from entities in the outer darkness in relation to Emily's strange behaviour towards me (and to at least one other person whom she knew quite well for many years) invites a consideration of the wide, controversial topic of deliverance in relation to healing. I myself have been under attack on a number of occasions, and so have no doubt about the reality of the danger. But if one is centred on Christ, centred on the sacramental life of one's particular church, and centred on unceasing prayer, one has little to fear. It is those who have a natural psychic sensitivity and prefer to work on their own without reference to the authority of the Church who are especially at risk of attack. The removal of an invading entity is in most cases not difficult provided one commands it to go in the name of the Creator, the Holy Trinity, and with the power of Christ. Unfortunately, as Jesus warned his disciples, the invasion is very likely to be repeated unless there is a radical change of heart, a metanoia, a true conversion to the light of God's countenance, on the part of the oppressed person. There must also be no further dabbling in the occult by such a person. The occult, or hidden, sphere is not necessarily more evil than the overt dimension, but unfortunately its evil side is more easily veiled from rational scrutiny. In all deliverance work, love is the most important quality, a love for the invading entity no less than for its victim. In the end the displaced power has to be directed to its proper situation in the life eternal, primarily the life beyond death, which God has prepared for its reception and ultimate healing. It, too, is a creature of God, no matter how aberrant its behaviour may be or how misplaced its situation. God in his infinite wisdom no doubt has work planned for it also. In the ministry of love the aggressor is in need of help no less than its victim, but a long time may have to elapse for the culprit to be recognized and his release secured.

Love tends to expose harmful psychic presences, which may then seek a new life under the protective power of the Almighty. Quite a number of instances of disturbing psychic phenomena involving property are caused by deceased 'spirits' seeking release from their burden of guilt due to misconduct when they were incarnate in that very environment. To seek forgiveness is to attain it, but unless there is a sincere repentance and a commitment to lead a new life of loving service, the problem will recur indefinitely. Thus, as stated above, total release may take a long time, if we dare extrapolate terrestrial time to the psychic dimension with any degree of accuracy. The same principle applies to absolution and forgiveness of sin in our much more restricted earthly sphere: the proof of forgiveness of sin is the lessened tendency to commit the same sin until eventually the life of the penitent is completely blameless – at least with regard to the fault in question, but ultimately of all faults. This final situation is certainly beyond earthly time, and cannot be separated from the collective sin of the world, since we are all parts of the one body of humanity.

Since God is love and therefore cherishes everything he has created, what happens to species of life that have become extinct? This question is clearly outside our knowledge – the rationalist would sneer at the simple-mindedness of any normal person even posing such a question, since extinction is surely synonymous with total annihilation. My own intimation is that although the form is indeed annihilated, the energy, or spirit, within it has now been diverted to a new creation, of greater pertinence to the universal situation than it was in a previous dispensation. Within the last two decades the virus of smallpox has been eliminated from the entire world, so that this terrible scourge is now merely an historical curiosity. A newcomer during this time has been the unrelated virus of AIDS, but perhaps some of the smallpox virus' power has also been diverted into more constructive patterns of activity in the great world of nature around us. The thought is stimulating even if the answer is far beyond our reckoning. Everything that God created is intrinsically good, but its descent into the world of desire, analogous to the Fall described in Genesis 3, brings it into the place of choice, of free will. It is then that the antitheses of good and evil arise. The responsibility of the human species in our little world is frightening, for we control the remainder of creation here. What effect our thoughts and especially our prayers have on the cosmic level, God alone knows. It is certainly a great privilege to know human emotions, but the responsibility for their proper direction is something we all have to learn. We look forward to the day when St Paul's proclamation will be fully actualized: 'There is no such thing as Jew or Greek, slave or freeman, male or female; for you are all one person in Christ Jesus' (Galatians 3:28). When one considers the terrible divisions within the Christian Church two thousand years later, one has to acknowledge the slow progress of love in the world community.

11

Fulfilment

This account of the deeper implications of the healing process began with the ministry of three people with an outstanding, though quite individual, gift. It seems right to consider their end and what they bequeathed to others in the hope that we who follow on may continue their work which has ignited the divine flame within us. The Holy Spirit is unceasingly about his business of renewing all things by a creative act that transmutes the old order, establishing it in the light of a continuing revelation.

Constance Peters, whose ministry released me from an incapacitating nasal obstruction and led me in the direction of my own spiritual work, succeeded so well in her own endeavours that her Science of Life Fellowship, supported by an excellent Bible-based newsletter, was able to acquire more spacious quarters. She was therefore able to leave her rather cramped flat and move into a fine detached house in a decidedly more attractive part of London. However, the expansion brought its own problems along with it. There were disagreements among the committee which insidiously undermined the Fellowship, and the roar of aircraft overhead at peak hours of travel (the house, unbeknown to the committee at the time of purchase, lay in the direct route of aircraft flying to and from London's great international airport) disturbed the peace of the place. Nevertheless, Constance's work continued with a devoted group of friends, and the Sunday meditation-healing service was especially beautiful. In the midst of her work she was suddenly assailed by an agonizing pain in the chest, and she died a few hours later. Thus it was that a dedicated healing ministry of many years' duration was brought to an abrupt end by a severe heart attack.

Her death occurred twelve years after my own healing in the church at Brighton. Many of her past associates had moved far from her both in locality and in the sphere of their interests, but her funeral was very well attended by many who had been close to her in the past. One could, nevertheless, not fail to sense the loneliness of a woman – the essence of affability and fun as she was – who was greatly separated in spirit from those around her. Gifts isolate, no matter how generous one may be in their bestowal on others. The work of the Fellowship was continued for a time by an especially close friend from a base outside London, but after a few years it ceased in that form. Many still have cause to remember Constance with gratitude.

Mary Macaulay, the courageous voice of spiritual truth in psychological and social trends, was also to see her Iona Education Centre grind gradually to a halt. It was her defect in not being able to delegate her teaching work to her followers that brought about this decline, though it must be admitted that few of them could have assumed the full burden of her ministry or have spoken with her unique authority. The 1960s were times of extreme social, psychological and spiritual experimentation, and Mary's approach was too traditional for the radical element while far too adventurous for both professional educationalists in colleges and workers in religious institutions. She was often her own worst enemy in her inability to understand the qualms of intelligent critics. As the centre failed to attract visitors, so she lost heart and consoled herself by eating far too much when she was alone. This was, of course, a compensation for her terrible feeling of frustration as she witnessed her creation wither away through the sheer indifference of the outside world. She became increasingly overweight, her blood pressure rose to a dangerously high level, and in due course she suffered a massive stroke that left the right side of her body paralysed and her speech reduced to gibberish.

Mary spent nearly two years in a nursing home for incapacitated old people, where she was greatly loved. The erstwhile impatience, irritation and resentment that had so marred her happiness and peace of mind yielded to a mute acceptance of life around her. She flowed out in love to all who knew her, nurses and fellow-patients alike. Even holding her hand seemed to impart a blessing from her, and the other patients enjoyed visiting her. The unhappy, querulous old woman of the past had matured into a being of warmth and light, the very model of the fully actualized person she had envisaged in her only book called *Understanding Ourselves*. It has long been out of print, and in any case much of its message is now a part of social teaching and spiritual guidance – at least in the work of enlightened educationalists and ministers of religion. There were many points of contact between her views and those of well-known psychoanalysts, except that she was not afraid to stress the spiritual component of personality and its possible development in the life beyond death.

It is, however, one thing to write about spiritual and emotional maturity and another to practise it in the harsh environment of the dissonant, insensitive society around one. What she could not do when still active she put into practice with great poignancy in her childlike openness as she lay helpless in bed murmuring her strangely attractive, unintelligible, babbling language which was punctuated by words that could with difficulty be identified. I always recall 'boysan girls' and 'bisher-bosher', which succeeded the first words as she grew weaker. When she died there was a sense of mourning for her in the home. The nursing staff knew they had lost a source of love whose radiance illuminated so much of the heavy ritual of caring for patients with senile dementia and other degenerative conditions of the brain, to say nothing of the equally tragic diseases of the limbs and joints that so immobilize elderly patients. In those days, joint-replacement operations were very much in the experimental stage.

The centre closed soon after her death. It had been maintained by the devotion of Freda, who could not bear the thought of Mary recovering sufficiently to continue her work and finding nowhere to go. On one level this was pathetic sentimentality – as if the victim of a stroke of such severity could ever recover sufficiently to lead an independent existence! But it was in fact a measure of Freda's great love, incapacitated as she was by her poor vision and generally feeble condition. I often feel that Mary's mantle fell on my shoulders and that I am the true inheritor and propagator of her wisdom. To be sure, I have progressed in my own thinking and practice since those far-off days (she died in 1971), and yet the older I become, the more often do I find that my words are a development of her themes rather than a new trend of thought. But who can claim an absolute originality for any idea, since the Holy Spirit alone is the true source! She was an innovator in her own particular field, and the ultimate fruit of her largely disregarded labours will be seen in the lives of generations to come. We may hope that the experimental permissiveness of the 1960s and the somewhat intolerant conformist trends of the 1980s will eventually attain a balance, even a synthesis, through inspired spiritual instruction of the type that Mary pioneered from the period of the Second World War up to the time of her death some thirty years later. I am frequently aware of her spiritual presence encouraging me in my own solitary path as I proclaim the message in speech and writing.

Ronald Beesley, who initiated me decisively into the healing ministry, has remained the most shadowy of my three mentors. I lost contact with him several years after my two weeks' stay at his healing centre which he called the 'College of Psychotherapeutics'. I was less close to him, either emotionally or spiritually, than to Mary and Constance. His healing centre was some distance away from London, and his phenomenal psychic powers were peripheral to my particular way: a devotion to spiritual growth as expounded by the world's great mystical tradition, the perennial philosophy that we have already considered. I continued to hear about the fine work he was doing in healing and psychic counselling and also as a teacher of increasing stature. An impressive body of disciples followed him, and he took groups of them to centres of spiritual power in Europe and the Holy Land. I never felt any special inclination to follow him either in his healing practice or on his travels, much as I revered his expertise and rejoiced in his assistance to so many different types of people. And yet I was never far from his warm, healing presence, no matter how much our paths might have diverged. He died tragically in a road-traffic accident when he and a group of his followers were on tour in India. I have heard it said that he had had misgivings about this particular tour – one among so many in his active life – but in the end he decided to go. It is clear that the die was cast before the journey, and he went to his death with his usual courage and good humour. His work continues to be propagated by some of his closest associates. I am told that they are doing very good work both in teaching and healing. However, a psychic genius of Ronald's stature would be hard to emulate. Gifts come from God, but teaching can be perpetuated by human sources in contact with the master.

The life of Jesus illustrates this principle especially well, except that his teaching, transmitted by an oral tradition, is sometimes fragmented and also probably excessively biased against the Pharisees who, after all, were the bastions of the Jewish spirituality of that time, and whose views, especially concerning the life of the world to come, had features in common with that of the early Christian proclamation. On the one hand, the written law is more immediately authoritative than the oral tradition, but on the other it can be so revered in its own right that it is in danger of becoming a prison rather than a way of life. I personally do not regret that Jesus left us no authentic written records, for he too was a child of his particular time and place and therefore inevitably subject to its limitations. This is the meaning of incarnation and also its price. But the essence of his teachings is eternally true. 'The written law condemns to death, but the Spirit gives life' (2 Corinthians 3:6).

When I meditate upon the lives of these three gifted people, I sense that their loneliness was profound even when they were surrounded by crowds of admirers. My thoughts go back also to Jesus' isolation even in the midst of his well-meaning but obtuse disciples. He said to one doctor of the law who offered to follow him wherever he went, 'Foxes have holes, the birds their nests, but the Son of Man has nowhere to lay his head' (Matthew 8:19–20). In the collateral account of Luke 9:57–58, it is a man on the road who makes this offer of discipleship. I do not believe that Jesus is stressing the frugality of his life so much as its unceasing labour. He is out so frequently on his mission, and therefore either living rough or in somebody else's house, that he has no permanent home of his own. Though extremely well-known, he is yet essentially a visitor, indeed a stranger. So, of course, are we all during our brief sojourn in this world, but the spiritual pioneer can no longer hide himself among the throng. He has to stand out from it, proclaim his mission, and wait for acclaim, misunderstanding, death and final resurrection in the path of the One who shows the way: Jesus Christ (and all those who preceded him in the work of faith, whose actions are celebrated so unforgettably in Hebrews 11).

I myself was led quite ineluctably in the way of service to the Church as the fulfilment of my own healing ministry. It was in 1966 – five years before I was received into the Church – that I saw Ronald Beesley for what chanced to be the last time. He was the speaker at a weekend conference held at the country healing centre (mentioned in a previous chapter) to which Freda had invited him. (Freda was also a friend of Constance Peters; we all seemed to circulate in an orbit of kindred interests even though some paths rarely crossed.) We three were discussing some trivial matter when Ronald suddenly turned to me and said, 'Martin, don't get involved in religion'. I was stunned at this remark, because religion had always been at the centre of my awareness, and furthermore Ronald was himself a most religious man. In the lovely little chapel of White Lodge, where he lived and did his work at his 'College of Psychotherapeutics', he held a Friday evening healing service of a type similar to the one I have described which took place in the Brighton church when Constance Peters ministered so powerfully to me. We sang hymns from a mainstream Christian hymn-book (*Congregational Praise*).

Then he went around laying his hands on the heads of all those present, signing them with the sign of the cross on their foreheads (this applied equally to non-Christians, whether by ignorance, acceptance, or indifference, I have never discovered) at the end of his ministry to them.

But Ronald was alluding to sectarian religious commitment, for he was, quite understandably in view of the repeated rebuffs he had suffered from various ignorant parsons in his younger days, profoundly anti-clerical. He loved Christ but had no time for the ministers of the Church that had sprung up in Christ's name. How often can one sympathize with this point of view until one remembers that without the Church the tradition would have withered away, its contents being lost in the sands of time and covered in the mists of oblivion! He, with his gift of precognition (perhaps it had been mediated by an angelic presence in the world beyond death), saw the trend of my future life, and was appalled at its prospect of a narrowing of my vision as I became increasingly restricted within the carapace of prejudice of an ecclesiastical structure.

To be quite frank, as I have previously stated, this too was my misgiving when the stern portals of the Church loomed ever nearer and I finally prepared myself for ordination. All the qualms I had at that time have, fortunately, been proved groundless. While there are some within the Church who look askance at the least mention of the word 'psychic', the prejudice is gradually relaxing, except in fundamentalistic circles devoted to the literal word of Scripture without reference to the many social and intellectual advances that have been made since the Bible was compiled. However, in as broad a tradition as that of Anglicanism, various schools of thought rejoice in a freedom of expression and a privacy of judgement, so that each can learn to live and let live with ever-widening knowledge and deepening charity. The agonizing maturing process teaches us how much we still have to learn and how ephemeral is all theory that does not have love at its core. But until one has finally committed oneself to a definite stance, one is like an undecided traveller hoping vainly to arrive at some destination in due course. In fact, it is the commitment that determines the destination, but the traveller must be constantly aware of the need for changing course as greater knowledge comes to him.

Priesthood conferred on me a power of action and an authority of command that did not exist during the period of my service as a layman in the Church. Apart from the sacramental aspect of ordination, my total commitment enabled God to use me in an altogether more effective ministry. I look for the time when all believers will be priests, but this will happen only when the individual believer is as committed to the Faith as is the minister at the time of his or her own ordination. Then, indeed, God will be with us as an irrefutable inner and outer presence.

For the first seven years of my priesthood I functioned in a non-stipendiary capacity, but then in 1983 I was asked by my diocesan bishop to take charge of the church to which I had already been attached for five years. And so now I am priest-in-charge of a beautiful church behind the Albert Hall in London. The parish is small, comprising some colleges of higher education served by their own chaplains, an army barracks (again with its own chaplain), a small residential area, and much parkland. Nearly all my congregation comes from outside the parish boundaries, some travelling in from a considerable distance to join the worship on Sundays.

At the beginning of 1982, a year before I was made priest-in-charge, I together with my entire peer-group were prematurely retired (on account of stringent economizing) from the medical institute where we taught our various disciplines to postgraduate surgical students. It seems providential, from my point of view, that I was thus relieved of my medical work (though I still do a small amount of teaching in an honorary capacity, for pathology remains a deep love of mine), since I can now devote my efforts more fully to the ministry of healing, counselling, spiritual direction, and deliverance, as well as looking after the fine church that has been put in my charge and where I am supported by a body of devoted worshippers. When, however, I had to face imminent early retirement from my medical post, I felt as if fate had smartly slapped my face, and I was sorely tempted to accept

132

professional employment elsewhere. This would have been highly advantageous financially, but the familiar inner voice (at variance with the advice proffered by 'spiritual' friends) told me to devote my time in my own home to those who needed my special ministry: the medical work could be done by another pathologist, but my spiritual work was unique. I did not dare to dream at that time that soon a completely new responsibility was to be laid on my shoulders. My medical career has been, in fact, an essential apprenticeship for a healing ministry of a truly holistic character in which the scientific, psychic and sacramental elements can work side by side, to the greater glory of God.